NATIONS OF THE WORLD

SPAIN

Nathaniel Harris

www.raintreepublishers.co.uk
Visit our website to find out more information about **Raintree** books.

To order:
☎ Phone 44 (0) 1865 888113
📄 Send a fax to 44 (0) 1865 314091
💻 Visit the Raintree bookshop at **www.raintreepublishers.co.uk** to browse our catalogue and order online.

First published in Great Britain by Raintree, Halley Court, Jordan Hill, Oxford, OX2 8EJ, part of Harcourt Education Ltd.
Raintree is a registered trademark of Harcourt Education Ltd.

Copyright © 2004 The Brown Reference Group plc.
The moral right of the proprietor has been asserted.

Produced for Raintree by the Brown Reference Group plc
Project Editor: Dawn Titmus
Designer: Graham Curd
Picture Researcher: Susy Forbes
Cartographers: Mark Walker and Peter Bull
Editorial Assistant: Tom Webber
Indexer: Kay Ollerenshaw
Consultant: Clive Carpenter

Raintree Publishers
Editor: Kate Buckingham

Printed and bound in Singapore.

ISBN 1 844 43245 9
08 07 06 05 04
10 9 8 7 6 5 4 3 2 1

British Library cataloguing in publication data
Harris, Nathaniel
Spain
914.6
A full catalogue is available for this book from the British Library.

Acknowledgements
Front cover: Dancer at a Spanish festival
Title page: Windmills near Toledo, Spain

The acknowledgements on page 128 form part of this copyright page.

Every effort has been made to contact copyright holders of any material reproduced in this book. Any omissions will be rectified in subsequent printings if notice is given to the publishers.

Contents

Foreword

Since ancient times, people have gathered together in communities where they could share and trade resources and strive to build a safe and happy environment. Gradually, as populations grew and societies became more complex, communities expanded to become nations – groups of people who felt sufficiently bound by a common heritage to work together for a shared future.

Land has usually played an important role in defining a nation. People have a natural affection for the landscape in which they grew up. They are proud of its natural beauties – the mountains, rivers and forests – and of the towns and cities that flourish there. People are proud, too, of their nation's history – the shared struggles and achievements that have shaped the way they live today.

Religion, culture, race and lifestyle, too, have sometimes played a role in fostering a nation's identity. Often, though, a nation includes people of different races, beliefs and customs. Many may have come from distant countries. Nations have rarely been fixed, unchanging things, either territorially or racially. Throughout history, borders have changed, often under the pressure of war, and people have migrated across the globe in search of a new life or because they are fleeing from oppression or disaster. The world's nations are still changing today: some nations are breaking up and new nations are forming.

Although Spain is part of Europe, it is also cut off from the rest of the continent by the Pyrenees mountains. Spain's isolation has created unique traditions, such as bullfighting. However, when the Spanish created a large empire in the so-called New World in the 16th and 17th centuries, they took their traditions with them. Spanish culture, architecture and language are still familiar throughout Mexico and much of Central and South America. For centuries, Spain was a relatively poor agricultural nation. Political upheavals in the 20th century further restricted development, but Spain has emerged as a modern nation and taken its place as a major player in the European Union.

Introduction

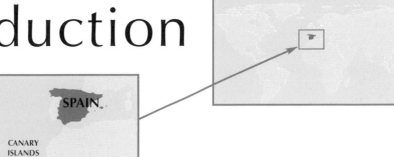

Mainland Spain is located in the south-west corner of Europe, occupying most of the Iberian peninsula. It shares the peninsula with its much smaller western neighbour, Portugal, and, to the south, Gibraltar, which is a British colony. Two groups of islands and two tiny areas on the coast of north Africa are also part of the Kingdom of Spain. The coasts of mainland Spain face both the Atlantic Ocean and the Mediterranean Sea. France lies to the north, across the snow-capped Pyrenees and the tiny independent principality of Andorra. To the south, across the Strait of Gibraltar, looms the continent of Africa.

These geographical links have subjected Spain to a great variety of influences and sent Spaniards travelling in all directions – into the Mediterranean, out across the Atlantic, south into Africa and – with greater difficulty because of the barrier of the Pyrenees – north into Europe. As a result, the character and customs of Spain became rather different from those of other European countries, most obviously in traditional activities such as bullfighting and flamenco song and dance.

For better or worse, traditional ideas and customs have lost much of their influence in Spain today. In particular, religion, formerly a dominant force, plays a smaller part in most people's lives. Factors such as membership of the European Union (EU) and the growth

Most of Spain's population lives in towns and cities. Barcelona, pictured here, is the country's second-largest city.

FACT FILE

- Spain has one of the lowest fertility rates in the world, with 1.13 children born per woman.

- There are nearly 500,000 Roma (Gypsies) in Spain. Most of them live in Andalusia.

- Spain is one of Europe's least densely populated countries, with 81 people per sq km (210 per sq mile).

- Four-fifths of Spain's citizens live in towns and cities.

- Spain is divided into nineteen autonomous communities (*comunidades autónomas*), most of which are further divided into provinces. Each community has its own parliament.

of mass tourism have helped to bring the Spanish way of life closer to those of its neighbours. Though it retains certain distinctive features, Spain is now a modern country in which the majority of its citizens live hectic, city-based lives.

NAME AND MONEY

Spain's official name is the Kingdom of Spain, or Spain for short (España in Spanish). It is a **parliamentary monarchy**. The king is the head of state, and the head of the government, called the president, is the leader of the political party that wins the most votes. After the Spanish Civil War (1936–39), Spain was ruled by a dictator, General Francisco Franco (see page 75), who enforced traditional values. After Franco's death in 1975, the monarchy was brought back, and in 1978, a full democratic system was established.

Spain joined the EU in 1986, and in 2002 it adopted the single currency of the EU, the euro, as its national currency. Before that time, the Spanish currency was the peseta. There are 100 cents to the euro. Banknotes are printed in 500, 200, 100, 50, 20, 10 and 5 euros. Coins are minted for 2 euros and 1 euro, as well as for 50, 20, 10, 5, 2 and 1 cent. Euro banknotes are the same throughout the EU, but the coins have one common side and one national side. Spain's euro coins feature images important Spanish people and places. The 10, 20 and 50-cent coins, for example, depict Miguel de Cervantes, the father of Spanish literature (see page 95).

THE PEOPLE OF SPAIN

Just under 41 million people live in Spain. This is not a large number in relation to the country's size, even allowing for the large areas that are mountainous and

The EU's single currency, the euro, replaced the peseta as Spain's national currency in 2002. The banknotes are the same across the EU, while the coins differ among countries.

POPULATION DENSITY

Large areas of Spain are sparsely populated, particularly in the centre of the country. The largest cities – Madrid, Barcelona, Valencia and Seville – and parts of the north-west, the Costa del Sol and the Canary and Balearic islands are the most densely populated regions.

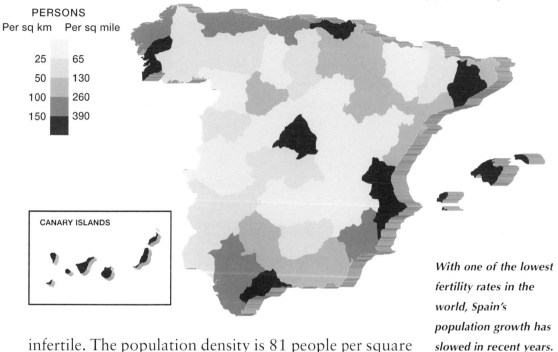

PERSONS

Per sq km	Per sq mile
25	65
50	130
100	260
150	390

CANARY ISLANDS

With one of the lowest fertility rates in the world, Spain's population growth has slowed in recent years.

infertile. The population density is 81 people per square kilometre (210 per square mile), compared with 241 people per square kilometre (624 per square mile) in the UK. Furthermore, the population is very unevenly distributed, since almost 80 per cent of Spaniards are crowded into the towns and cities.

Until recently, Spain was primarily an agricultural country, but economic changes encouraged millions to move from the countryside to the cities. As a result, some remote areas are virtually uninhabited. There are also about a million recent immigrants in Spain, the majority from north Africa but some also from Latin America.

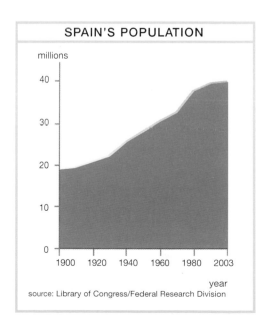

SPAIN'S POPULATION

millions

source: Library of Congress/Federal Research Division

9

Spain's mountain ranges meant that communications between different regions were difficult until modern times. This encouraged the development of strong regional loyalties, especially since Spain was only united into a single country near the end of the 15th century. Encouraged by the divisions, distinctive regional identities persisted over the centuries and often challenged the authority of the central government.

The present Spanish Constitution recognizes seventeen regions, known as autonomous communities, each of which runs most of its own affairs. Asturias and the Basque Country in the north, Castile in central Spain, Aragon in the east and its north-eastern neighbour, Catalonia, are among the communities that have had a separate existence in the past and today still retain a very distinctive character.

National symbols

Spain's national anthem is 'La Marcha Real' ('The Royal March'), by an unknown composer. There are no words. The national flag consists of three horizontal bands coloured red, yellow and red. On state occasions, a coat of arms appears in the centre of the flag. The Pillars of Hercules (Gibraltar and Ceuta, the 'rocks' jutting out into the Strait of Gibraltar) feature on one side. The coat of arms carries symbols of Castile, León, Aragon, Navarre and Granada – Spanish states that were joined together over time to form the present kingdom. Each of the country's seventeen autonomous communities also has its own flag.

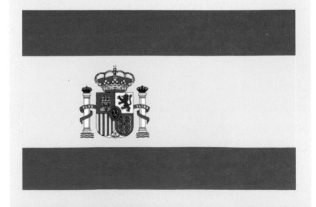

LANGUAGES AND RELIGION

What we call Spanish is the language of Castile. Today, about three-quarters of the people in Spain speak Castilian Spanish, but three other languages are widely used and are officially recognized in their home areas – Catalan (17 per cent of speakers), Galician (7 per cent) and Basque, or Euskera (2 per cent).

The language of the Basques is a mystery. Most

WHERE DOES SPAIN'S POPULATION LIVE?

78% cities and towns

22% countryside

European and some Asian languages belong to a group known as the Indo-European languages. However unalike they may seem, they are all related. But Euskera does not belong to the Indo-European group and is not related to any other known language. It is believed to date back to a time before Indo-European speakers entered Europe. This suggests that the Basques may be the descendants of a people who settled in Spain and south-west France before most other present-day peoples arrived in Europe.

Spain's other three official languages – Spanish, Catalan and Galician – are Latin tongues that evolved from the speech of the ancient Romans. Catalan is the language of Catalonia, the affluent region in the north-east of Spain, and Galician, or Gallego, is the language of Galicia, in the far north-west of Spain. Some dialects (that is more localized versions of languages spoken by smaller numbers of people), such as Valencian, are also spoken.

About 93 per cent of Spaniards describe themselves as Roman Catholic, but nearly a third of that total do not go to church or otherwise practice their faith. Seven per cent of Spaniards belong to other religions.

Like many industrialized nations, Spain has an increasingly ageing population – 17 per cent of people are aged 65 or older.

RELIGIOUS PERSUASION

%
65 Roman Catholic
28 non-practising Catholic
7 other

Source: *CIA Factbook, 2003*

LANGUAGE GROUPS

%
74 Castilian Spanish
17 Catalan
7 Galician
2 Basque

Source: *CIA Factbook, 2003*

POPULATION BY AGE

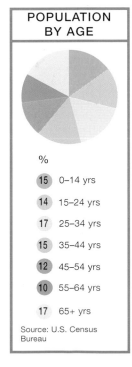

%
15 0–14 yrs
14 15–24 yrs
17 25–34 yrs
15 35–44 yrs
12 45–54 yrs
10 55–64 yrs
17 65+ yrs

Source: U.S. Census Bureau

11

Land and cities

'To Cordoba belong all the beauty and ornaments that delight the eye or dazzle the sight'.

19th-century English historian Stanley Lane-Poole

Spain is the second-largest country in western Europe after France. It covers an area of 504,782 square kilometres (194,896 square miles), which includes the Balearic and Canary islands and the towns of Ceuta and Melilla on the north African coast.

Spain was relatively isolated from the rest of Europe until recent times, mainly because of the Pyrenees mountain range running across the top of the peninsula. The Pyrenees formed a barrier to trade, travel and even the spread of certain species of wildlife, and this accounts for some of the country's unique characteristics and customs. For a long time, Spain's geography also created obstacles that accentuated regional differences.

Spain is the fourth-highest European country after Switzerland, Austria and Norway. It mostly consists of a high central plateau, the meseta, averaging 610 metres (2000 feet) above sea level. The plateau is crossed and also surrounded by mountain ranges. The major rivers flow through basins between the mountains. Four great rivers, the Guadalquivir, the Duero, the Tajo (Tagus) and the Guadiana, flow from east to west into the Atlantic Ocean. The fifth, the Ebro, flows in the other direction, into the Mediterranean Sea.

The variety of the terrain, and the presence of two very different bodies of water on its coasts – the Atlantic and the Mediterranean – have helped to make Spain

Almonds are grown on the coastal plain in the south and south-east of Spain, as this orchard in Alicante province shows.

FACT FILE

● Mainland Spain's highest peak is Mulhacén (3482 m or 11,420 ft) in the Sierra Nevada. The highest point in Spanish territory is Pico de Teide (3718 m or 12,198 ft). It is on the island of Tenerife in the Canary Islands.

● Spain covers nearly 84% of the Iberian peninsula.

● The meseta – the tableland in the centre of the country– covers 40% of mainland Spain.

● In Spain, the Bay of Biscay is called the Mar Cantábrico (Cantabrian Sea).

● Parts of Spain, such as Valladolid on the northern meseta, receive very little rainfall.

The Cordillera Bética, a mountain range in southern Andalusia, runs east into Murcia, plunges into the Mediterranean Sea and emerges after 200 km (125 miles) to form the islands of Ibiza and Majorca.

a land of extremes of soil, climate and wildlife. In the 21st century, these features are still very much in evidence. Spain is a modern country with an advanced industrial economy, and almost four-fifths of its people live in towns and cities. Thanks to the country's size and the fact that it has a small, largely urban population, very large areas of the countryside – as well as the wildlife that inhabits them – are free from human interference to an extent that is unusual in Europe.

GEOGRAPHICAL REGIONS

Although the Spanish landscape is unusually varied by European standards, the mainland can be divided into five large geographical regions. These are the northern mountains, the meseta, the Ebro basin, the Mediterranean coastal plain and the Guadalquivir basin.

SPAIN'S LANDFORMS

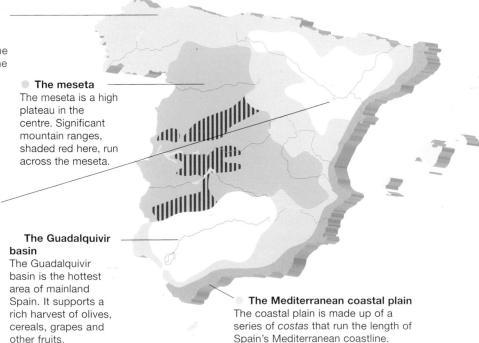

Mountain regions
The Cordillera Cantábrica and the Pyrenees run across the north of the country, the Sistema Ibérica is located north-east of the mesta and the Cordillera Bética runs south of the Guadalquivir basin.

The meseta
The meseta is a high plateau in the centre. Significant mountain ranges, shaded red here, run across the meseta.

The Ebro basin
The River Ebro flows south-east into the Mediterranean. This is a dry region, and the river is used to irrigate some areas.

The Guadalquivir basin
The Guadalquivir basin is the hottest area of mainland Spain. It supports a rich harvest of olives, cereals, grapes and other fruits.

The Mediterranean coastal plain
The coastal plain is made up of a series of *costas* that run the length of Spain's Mediterranean coastline.

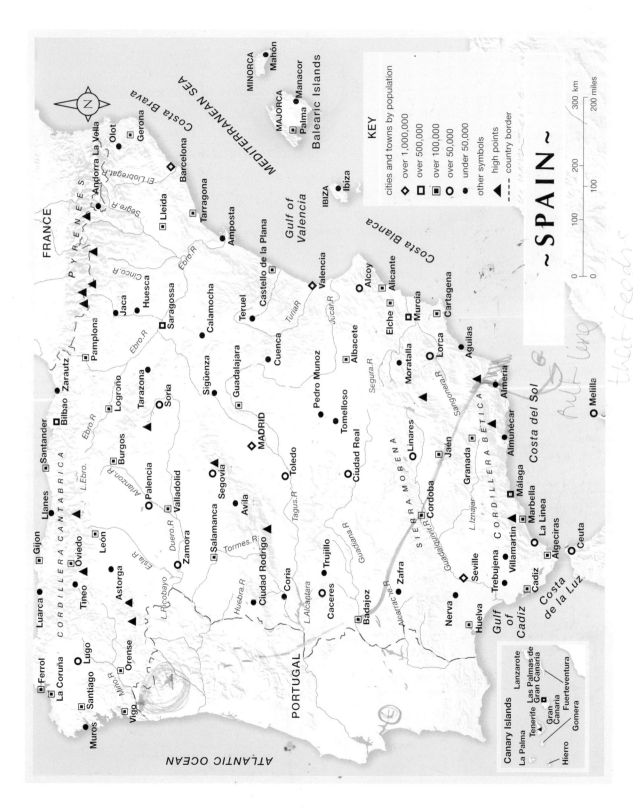

~SPAIN~

KEY

cities and towns by population

◇ over 1,000,000
□ over 500,000
▣ over 100,000
○ over 50,000
● under 50,000

other symbols

▲ high points
- - - country border

0   100   200   300 km

0   100   200 miles

MEDITERRANEAN SEA

Costa Brava

MINORCA   Mahón

MAJORCA   Manacor
Palma   Balearic Islands

IBIZA   Ibiza

Gulf of Valencia

Costa Blanca

FRANCE

Andorra La Vella   Olot
Gerona
PYRENEES   El Llobregat.R
Segre.R   Barcelona
Lleida   Tarragona
Jaca   Amposta
Huesca
Cinca.R
Pamplona   Saragossa
Ebro.R   Calamocha   Castello de la Plana
Zarautz   Tarazona   Teruel   TuriaR
Bilbao   Logroño   Soria   Cuenca   Valencia
Santander   Burgos   Sigüenza   JucarR   Alcoy
Llanes   Palencia   Guadalajara   Segura.R   Alicante
Gijón   Valladolid   MADRID   Pedro Munoz   Albacete   Elche   Murcia   Cartagena
Oviedo   León   Segovia   Toledo   Tomelloso   Moratalla   Lorca   Aguilas
Luarca   Tineo   Astorga   Avila   Ciudad Real   SangoneraR   Almeria
CORDILLERA CANTABRICA   Zamora   Salamanca   SIERRA MORENA   Linares   SangonetaR   Costa del Sol
L.Ebro.   Arlanzon.R   Tormes.R   Jaén   Granada   Almuñécar
Esla.R   Ciudad Rodrigo   Coria   Tagus.R   Cordoba   Malaga
Duero.R   Huebra.R   Guadiana.R   Guadalquivir.R   Marbella   CORDILLERA BÉTICA
L.Ricobayo   Trujillo   Alcantara   L.Iznajar   Villamartin   La Linea
Ferrol   Lugo   Orense   L.Alcantara   Zafra   Seville   Trebujena   Algeciras   Ceuta
La Coruña   Miño.R   Caceres   Badajoz   Nerva   Cadiz   Costa
Santiago   Vigo   Huelva   Gulf   de la Luz
Muros   PORTUGAL   of
Cadiz

Melilla

ATLANTIC OCEAN

Canary Islands

La Palma   Lanzarote
Tenerife   Las Palmas de Gran Canaria
Gran Canaria   Fuerteventura
Hierro   Gomera

The meseta is surrounded by mountains on all sides except the west. In the west, the meseta slopes gently down across Portugal.

The Balearic Islands in the Mediterranean Sea and the Canary Islands in the Atlantic Ocean also have distinctive geographic features.

The northern mountains

This region comprises the northern coast and the Pyrenees as far as the Mediterranean. Mountain ranges extend across it with hardly a break. The Galician Mountains in the west are succeeded by the Cantabrians, and then by the Pyrenees in the east. The coastline faces the Atlantic, and there are heavy rains when ocean winds sweep into the mountains. As a result, the region has a very distinctive character – milder, wetter and greener than the rest of Spain.

The western ranges rise to about 2400 metres (8000 feet) and are green and heavily wooded, with many rushing streams. The soil is generally poor here, and farmers prefer to raise grazing animals than grow crops. Coves and sandy beaches are found along the coast, but in many places, the mountains come right down to the sea. Galicia in particular has a dramatic coastline of sheer cliffs and beautiful inlets that have often been likened to the famous fiords of Norway. Fishing villages dot the coastline, and ports such as La Coruña, Vigo, Santander and Bilbao are evidence of the region's strong seafaring tradition.

The meseta

The meseta covers about 40 per cent of mainland Spain. It is a central plateau that rises between 400 and 1000 metres (1300 and 3300 feet) above sea level. Except in the west, it is surrounded by mountain ranges that rise to greater heights, so that it resembles a vast bowl.

The meseta consists of rolling plains, but these are broken in many places by hills or mountains. The most imposing chains are the near-continuous Sierra de Gredos and Sierra de Guadarrama, which extend roughly south-west to north-east across the centre of the meseta, from Portugal to the north-east of Madrid. The highest peak is the Plaza de Almanzor at 2592 metres (8501 feet). The southern boundary of the meseta is formed by another, lower mountain range, the Sierra Morena. Beyond it lies the higher Sierra Nevada, where the tallest peak in mainland Spain, Mount Mulhacén, reaches a height of 3482 metres (11,420 feet).

Though most of Spain's rivers rise in the meseta, the land itself is arid, which historically created severe problems for Spain. The plain is mostly scrubland, covered by shrubs and short grasses. Hot and dry in summer and often freezing in winter, the meseta was for centuries largely given over to sheep-farming. Like many parts of Spain, it is thinly populated outside the cities. A number of these cities – above all, the nation's capital, Madrid – are major population centres.

Much of the meseta is sparsely populated and is used for growing cereals. These windmills are located near Toledo, south of Madrid.

The Ebro basin

The Ebro is Spain's longest river (the Tajo is longer, but about a third of its length flows through Portugal). It is also the only major river in Spain that empties into the Mediterranean. It rises in the Cantabrian Mountains, to the south of the city of Santander, and travels east-south-eastwards for 910 kilometres (565 miles), plunging through deep gorges as it approaches the coast and then spreading out through a delta before it joins the sea. On its way, the river fertilizes the soil – for example at La Rioja, where the vineyards on the river banks produce famous wines. Generally, though, the Ebro basin is a dry region, and the river has long been used to irrigate some areas. In recent times, it has been

An isolated farm house stands among reed beds in the Ebro delta. The River Ebro fans out into a delta before emptying into the Mediterranean. The delta is located on the coast about halfway between Barcelona and Valencia.

increasingly exploited as a resource, and 35 large dams have been constructed as part of hydroelectric schemes.

The Ebro delta occupies an area of about 320 square kilometres (120 square miles). Silt brought down by the river has enlarged it over time, and now it thrusts out into the sea like an arrow head for 20 kilometres (12 miles). Much of the delta is given over to growing rice and other crops, but its lagoons, reedbeds and dunes also make it an important haven for waterbirds.

The Guadalquivir basin

Spain's second-longest river (657 kilometres or 408 miles) rises close to the Sierra Nevada in the south-east and flows westwards through the fertile southern region of Andalusia. This is also the hottest part of Spain. It is still strongly associated with the **Moors**, a people from North Africa who settled there for centuries, naming it al Andalus. Cordoba, one of the capitals of Moorish

Spain, stands beside the Guadalquivir. Further west, the river flows through another historic city, Seville, in the south-west, before reaching the marshes of the Doñana National Park and emptying into the Atlantic at the Gulf of Cadiz. The Guadalquivir basin is outstandingly rich in wildlife as well as supporting the cultivation of abundant grapes, olives, citrus fruits and cereals.

The Mediterranean coastal plain

There are low-lying areas on the Atlantic coasts of Spain, notably the Costa del Luz (Coast of Light), in the south-west between Tarifa and Cadiz. But the Mediterranean coastal plain is much longer and more continuous, running from the Pyrenees to Gibraltar. It is generally divided into a series of 'coasts'. From north to south, there are: the Costa Brava, the Costa Dorada, the Costa del Azahar, the Costa Blanca, the Costa Cálida, the Costa de Almería and the Costa del Sol.

There are wild areas along this coastline, mainly on the Costa Brava. The large stretches of sandy beaches, combined with warm seas and a sunny climate, have led to the growth of mass tourism and the development of resorts such as Benidorm, Torremolinos and Marbella. Along the east coast there are also two major ports, Barcelona and Valencia, which originally grew because of jobs created by trading opportunities in the Mediterranean. Further commercial and industrial growth in recent times has made Barcelona and Valencia the nation's second and third most populous cities.

As its name suggests, the Costa Brava (Rugged Coast) has some wild stretches of coastline. There are also some picturesque headlands and pretty inlets, such as this one in Gerona province.

The Balearic Islands

This group of islands lies in the western Mediterranean about 200 kilometres (125 miles) from the Spanish coast.

The Pyrenees

Running for some 430 kilometres (270 miles) between the Bay of Biscay and the Mediterranean, the Pyrenees are shared between Spain and France. In most places, the border runs along the crests of the highest mountains.

The small independent principality of Andorra lies at the very heart of the central Pyrenees. In this area, the mountains are permanently snow-capped, commonly rising above 2750 m (9000 ft). Among them stands the highest peak in the Pyrenees, Pico de Aneto, at 3404 m (11,168 ft).

Winters in the central Pyrenees are very severe, and in the valleys, the main occupation is sheep and cattle-grazing. Agriculture is more successful in the valleys at the western and eastern ends of the Pyrenees, which have milder Atlantic and Mediterranean climates. The dramatic appeal of the Pyrenees is enhanced by streams, waterfalls and passes over 1525 m (5000 ft), such as Somport and Poterla. The Pass of Roncesvalles, though lower at 1090 m (3576 ft), is even more famous in legend (see box on opposite page).

It comprises Majorca (in Spanish, Mallorca), Minorca, Cabrera, Ibiza, Formentera and a number of smaller islands. The largest, Majorca, has the most varied landscape, consisting of mountains with thickly forested sides as well as rolling, fertile countryside and the long, sandy beaches on which its booming tourist industry is based. Olives, citrus fruits and other Mediterranean crops are grown in the interior, but most of the population has been drawn to the coast to work in jobs created by tourism. Tourism also dominates the economies of Minorca and Ibiza. The chief cities of the Balearics are Palma, on Majorca, and Mahón, on Minorca.

The Canary Islands

There are seven major islands in this group: Tenerife, La Palma, La Gomera, El Hierro, Gran Canaria, Fuerteventura and Lanzarote. The Canaries lie in the Atlantic, over 1320 kilometres (820 miles) south-west of Spain – north Africa is closer at only 100 kilometres (60 miles) away. The islands were once ancient volcanoes, and the island beaches are made up of dark sand, the eroded remains of volcanic lava.

Tenerife has Spain's highest mountain, Pico de Teide, which rises to 3718 metres (12,198 feet). The largest city is Las Palmas on Gran Canaria. Thanks to the sub-tropical climate, crops such as bananas and coffee are grown in the Canaries, but the islands' year-round warmth has made tourism their principal industry.

THE AUTONOMOUS COMMUNITIES

Spain has always been a country of strong regional loyalties. Under Franco's long dictatorship (1939–75), however, local differences were ignored, and Castilian Spanish was the only recognized language. When **democracy** was established from 1975, there was a strong reaction in the other direction. Autonomy (self-government) was quickly granted to the historically distinct Basque and Catalan peoples, but there was continued pressure from other regions.

The 1978 Constitution made provision for Spain to be divided into nineteen autonomous communities. Political power is devolved (decentralized) to a remark-able degree, and each community has its own parliament. The autonomous communities are: in the far north, Galicia, Asturias, Cantabria, the Basque Country (País

The legend of Roncesvalles

According to a medieval French epic poem, *The Song of Roland*, the Frankish emperor Charlemagne conquered most of Spain. He then marched back to France through the Pass of Roncesvalles (now Roncevax) in the Pyrenees, where his rearguard was ambushed by a Moorish army. Led by Count Roland, the **Franks** fought to the last and Roland died heroically. Roland was a popular figure, and many legendary tales were told of him and his great friend, Olivier.

Roland was a real person who accompanied Charlemagne on his expedition to Spain in AD 778. But Charlemagne's conquests were limited to the north-east, and his rearguard was ambushed by Basques, not Moors.

AUTONOMOUS COMMUNITIES OF SPAIN

Spain is divided into seventeen autonomous communities (*comunidades autónomas*), each with its own parliament and powers of self-government. The city-enclaves of Ceuta and Melilla in Morocco also have some autonomy. For administrative purposes, the country is also subdivided into 50 provinces. The map shows the autonomous communities and capitals (marked •), as well as the provinces; unlabelled provinces share the name of the autonomous community.

AUTONOMOUS COMMUNITIES AND CAPITALS:

ANDALUSIA Seville
ARAGON Saragossa
ASTURIAS Oviedo
BALEARIC ISLANDS
  Palma de Mallorca
BASQUE COUNTRY
  Vitoria-Gasteiz
CANARY ISLANDS Las
  Palmas de Gran Canaria
CANTABRIA Santander
CASTILE AND LEON
  Valladolid
CASTILE-LA MANCHA
  Toledo
CATALONIA Barcelona
EXTREMADURA Merida
GALICIA Santiago de
  Compostela
LA RIOJA Logroño
MADRID Madrid
MURCIA Murcia
NAVARRE Pamplona
VALENCIA Valencia

Vasco) and Navarre; on the meseta, Castile and León, Madrid, Castile-La Mancha, Extremadura and La Rioja; to the east, Catalonia, Aragon, Valencia and Murcia; in the south, Andalusia; and outside the mainland, the Balearic Islands and Canary Islands. The city-enclaves of Ceuta and Melilla on the north African coast also have a limited autonomy.

Northern strongholds

The most northerly autonomous communities have a special character that largely results from the terrain and climate. These, in turn, influenced the history of the region. In the early 8th century AD, the northern mountains provided a refuge for Christian warriors, who were able to hold out against the advancing Moors. The region became a base for the Christian **Reconquest** of Spain (see page 58), but as the front line advanced, they lost their importance and became backwaters.

Galicia, in the far north-west, was so remote that it had little contact with the Moors. But at Santiago de Compostela, now the capital of Galicia, the shrine of St James became a symbol of the Reconquest. During the **Middle Ages**, it was also the most popular pilgrim site in western Europe, visited by thousands of people who travelled along well-marked pilgrim routes through France and northern Spain.

Neighbouring Asturias was formerly a separate kingdom. It offered the only successful resistance to the first wave of Moorish invaders, who are said to have been checked at Covadonga sometime between 718 and 725. Asturias is celebrated for its early medieval churches. The capital of the autonomous community is Oviedo.

In the early 20th century, the Spanish royal family took to spending the summer in Santander, making the elegant resort very fashionable. Today, the city is better known for its beaches and ferry connection to England.

The Romans occupied Segovia in 80 BC and built this impressive aqueduct. It was once 15 kilometres (10 miles) long and was constructed without the aid of mortar.

Cantabria's capital, Santander, became an elegant resort during the 19th century, but many of its fine old buildings were destroyed by fire in 1941. Among Cantabria's treasures are the prehistoric cave paintings at Altamira and the Picos de Europa, the spectacular mountain area Cantabria shares with Asturias and León.

The Basque Country (País Vasco in Castilian, or Euskadi in Basque) and Navarre are mainly inhabited by the Basque people. It appears they have asserted their independence in the western Pyrenees for thousands of years. An independent Basque kingdom of Navarre existed from the ninth to the sixteenth centuries. Basque language and culture were suppressed by Franco until democracy was restored after his death. The capital of the Basque Country is Vitoria, but the former industrial city of Bilbao and the coastal resort of San Sebastián are better known. Pamplona, capital of Navarre, is famous for 'the running of the bulls' each July, when the animals are released into the streets amid excited spectators.

The central communities

Castile and León is the largest of the autonomous communities, occupying over 94,220 square kilometres (36,380 square miles) of the northern meseta. León, in the north-west, was the chief Christian kingdom in Spain between the 10th and 13th centuries. In 1230, it was united with Castile, which then spearheaded the Reconquest and dominated a unified Spain. The name 'Castile' derives from the many castles (*castillos*) built in the region as part of the Reconquest. The historic cities of Castile include the capital, Valladolid, the university town of Salamanca, the old capital, Burgos, and

Segovia, which is celebrated for its 28-metre (92-foot) high Roman **aqueduct**.

Castile-La Mancha, also a very large autonomous community, represents territories acquired during a later phase of Castilian expansion. Before the setting up of the autonomous communities, Castile and León was known as Old Castile and Castile-La Mancha as New Castile. The capital of Castile-La Mancha is the city of Toledo. Between the two Castiles lie the Spanish capital, Madrid, and the area around it. This densely populated area forms a separate autonomous community.

To the south and west, Extremadura is rather bleak and remote. However, its capital, Mérida, was for a time the chief city of Roman Spain. Later, poverty seems to have spurred Extremadurans to play a leading role in the colonization of America. Both Hernán Cortés – the conqueror of Mexico – and Francisco Pizarro – the conqueror of Peru – came from the region.

Remote and picturesque villages, such as this one in Aragon, nestle among the high peaks of the Spanish Pyrenees.

There are Basque people in both Spain and France. While some Spanish Basques want an independent country, very few French Basques want to secede from (leave) France.

By contrast, La Rioja, east of the Castilian communities, is very small and more fertile in the valley of the Ebro River. Its capital, Logroño, lies on the Camino de Santiago, a pilgrims' way that traverses La Rioja and Castile and León before reaching the famous Galician shrine of Santiago de Compostela (see page 23).

Eastern Spain

Aragon stretches roughly north–south for 370 kilometres (230 miles) from the high Pyrenees to the thinly populated plateaux and mountains. Its capital, Zaragoza, is situated on the River Ebro and is a centre for important industries. Aragon was formerly a great kingdom, largely through a union with its wealthy, dynamic neighbour, Catalonia.

Catalonia occupies the north-east corner of Spain. Its coastline includes the rugged Costa Brava, the Ebro delta and, above all, its capital, Barcelona, which dominates the community. Catalonia has a long history as a commercial and maritime centre. It emerged as a buffer zone, set up in the 8th century by the **Frankish** empire of west-central Europe. Influences from beyond the Pyrenees strengthened a feeling of Catalan separateness from the rest of Spain that has lasted down to the present. United with Aragon from 1137, Catalonia became the driving force behind a medieval 'Aragonese' empire in the Mediterranean (see page 58).

Declining under the Spanish monarchy, in the 17th and 18th centuries Catalonia twice attempted to gain its independence. After it became industrialized in the 19th century, its subsequent history continued to be turbulent. Now autonomous, Catalonia remains consciously independent in outlook, despite the large numbers of non-Catalans who have come to live and work there.

The community of Valencia occupies the coastal plain and interior to the south of Catalonia. It is historically linked with Catalonia, and a local dialect, Valenciano, resembles Catalan. The capital, Valencia, was founded by the Romans in 138 BC and later became a flourishing Moorish city. It is on the coast, south of the Costa del Azahar. To the south, the Costa Blanca is one of Spain's greatest centres of package tourism. Its resorts, such as Benidorm, have often been criticized for being tastelessly overdeveloped.

Murcia lies on the coast immediately south-west of Valencia. It takes its name from its capital city, Murcia, a pre-Roman settlement refounded by the Moors in the ninth century. Although conquered by Castile in 1243, the region retains certain Moorish features such as canal systems. Even more ancient, the port of Cartagena owes its name to the Carthaginians. These settlers from the ancient north African city of Carthage founded the port in about 223 BC. Murcia's coast, the Costa Cálida, is known for its warm waters and is popular with Spanish visitors. The coast of Valencia and Murcia is often unofficially referred to as the Levante (Rising Sun).

The south

Andalusia is another historic region, now an autonomous community, with a highly distinctive character: Andalusians are generally seen as the most colourful and outward-going of Spaniards. Almost as large as Castile and León, Andalusia extends right across southern

A rocky outcrop rises above orchards and farmland in Andalusia. Much of the region is fertile, and grapes, citrus fruits and olives grow abundantly.

Spain from the Mediterranean to the Atlantic. Its size accounts for its notably varied features, although much of Andalusia consists of the Guadalquivir basin and the mountain ranges that run north and south of it. Among its cities are Cordoba and Granada – both rich in Moorish buildings – Málaga and the Atlantic port of Cadiz. The capital of Andalusia is another historic city, Seville (see page 44).

Agriculture and wine and sherry production remain the mainstays of the economy except along the coast. There, tourism generates huge revenues, and intensive development, long present on the Costa del Sol, has spread to other parts of the Andalusian coast including the Atlantic-facing Costa de la Luz.

The island communities

The autonomous community of the Balearics has been inhabited since prehistoric times. Early islanders left mysterious stone towers (*talayots*) and T-shaped pillars

Away from the busy tourist resorts on the coast, the sparsely populated interior of Majorca is made up of olive groves, pine forests and, in the north-west, rugged mountain ranges.

(*taulas*), created for some still unknown purpose. A long succession of occupiers followed, from the Romans onwards. The islands were conquered by Aragon in the 13th century, although Minorca was occupied by the British and French for periods in the eighteenth century. The capital of the Balearics is the Majorcan city, Palma de Mallorca, which has a historic cathedral and castle and many other fine buildings.

The Canary Islands were known in ancient times and were said to be notable for their many large dogs. The Spanish 'Canaria' derives from the Latin *canes*, meaning 'dogs'. The islands were not visited by Europeans until the late 14th century. The Spanish conquered them, and Christopher Columbus and other mariners used the Canaries as a springboard for Atlantic crossings to the Americas. The co-capital and chief port is Las Palmas on Gran Canaria.

The Guanches

When Europeans arrived in the Canary Islands late in the 14th century, they found them inhabited by a Stone Age people, the Guanches. Resisting the Spanish invaders, the Guanches were killed in large numbers and were wiped out by about 1600. They have left few traces behind, and little is known about them except for their practice of carefully mummifying their dead. One theory is that they were related to the Berbers of north Africa. On the island of La Gomera, a whistling 'language' survives that is said to have originated with the Guanches.

CLIMATE

Spain has 2600 hours of sunshine a year – more than any other country in Europe – which makes it a popular tourist destination. And as well as its geographical diversity, it has a varied climate that is more like that of the USA than other European countries.

One commonly used distinction is between 'wet' and 'dry' Spain. 'Wet' Spain is the temperate north and north-west. In these areas, cold northerly airstreams from the Atlantic bring heavy rains. The summers are cooler and the winters are milder compared to those in the rest of the country. La Coruña in Galicia, for example,

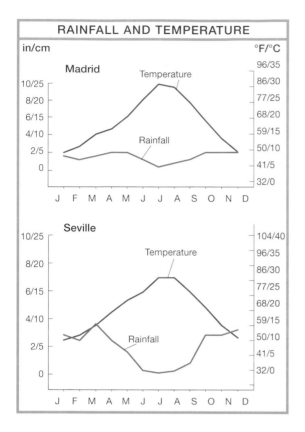

RAINFALL AND TEMPERATURE

Madrid

Seville

averages a temperature of 10 °C (51° F) in January and 19° C (66° F) in July. Annual rainfall is about 80 centimetres (32 inches). In Madrid, in the heart of the meseta, in January the average is 5° C (41° F), in July it is 25° C (77° F) and the average annual rainfall is 42 centimetres (17 inches). Averages can be misleading however, the Madrid climate, for example, can be extreme, with temperatures reaching 40° C (105° F) in summer and dipping below zero in winter.

Much of 'dry' Spain experiences similar climatic extremes. Throughout the meseta, hot, dry summers are followed by severe winters, often with blizzards. This is known as a continental climate and is typical of the interiors of land masses. The dryness of the meseta makes large areas unsuitable for agriculture, and many other parts of Spain have been threatened with drought despite extensive irrigation. However, there are local variations – for example, in western Andalusia, where Atlantic winds bring rain.

The coastal areas of the south and east have a Mediterranean climate – hot, dry summers and moist, mild winters. The Balearic islands also have a Mediterranean climate. The climate of the Canary Islands is subtropical, with little variation between summer and winter temperatures and little rainfall.

WILDLIFE AND PLANTS

Spain's varied terrain supports a greater variety of plant and animal life than any other European country. Its habitats include high mountains, scrub-covered plains, marshland and dry, sunny coasts. There is another reason for its abundant plant life, however. During the last Ice Age, Spain was only partly covered by glaciers, and many plants survived that were wiped out elsewhere in Europe. When the ice sheet retreated, the Pyrenees prevented such plants from spreading beyond Spain. As a result, there are around 5500 plant species that are unique to Spain, including exquisite orchids.

Plants and trees

Many small rock-climbing plants, including saxifrage and edelweiss, grow in the high mountain regions of mainland Spain. The mountain pastures below are filled

This restored waterwheel on the Guadalquivir River in Cordoba was originally constructed by the Moors. Long, dry summers mean that many rivers in southern Spain are seasonal, and therefore not suitable for generating power.

Spain is home to more than 8000 plant species, including species that are unique to Spain as well as more common ones, such as these poppies growing in a meadow.

with flowers such as gentians, crocuses, orchids and narcissi. Coniferous forests are found in most of the mountainous regions of Spain, and some are commercially managed for the timber industry. The silver fir is common, but the Spanish fir now grows naturally only in the Ronda area of Andalusia. There are many types of pine tree, including the striking umbrella pine, with its high, wide crown, which is usually found growing near the coast.

Deciduous forests of beech and Pyrenean oak grow on the cool lower slopes of the northern mountains, and plants such as bluebells, foxgloves and orchids carpet the ground. Areas of woodland with cork oaks and holm-oaks are found on the lowlands and plains. Both types of oak help to support Spanish farmers: the bark of the cork oak is stripped off about every ten years to be used for bottle corks, and the acorns of the holm-oak provide feed for domesticated pigs.

Arid scrubland is common throughout Spain. In places where natural forest has been cut down, plants such as heather, gorse and cistus have taken over. Herbs such as lavender, thyme and rosemary also grow well in this environment.

The Balearic Islands have a range of plant life similar to that of mainland Spain. However, because the islands have been separate from the mainland for thousands of years, species unique to the islands, such as the Balearic cyclamen, have also developed.

The plants of the Canary Islands include an unusual prickly-looking plant called the dragon tree.

Spain's rare animals

Spain's many wild and remote places offer a haven to several animals that have mostly disappeared from the rest of Europe. The brown bear lives in parts of Spain, but it has become endangered as a result of hunting and habitat destruction. In 1900, there were about a thousand bears in Spain, but now there are less than a hundred. They are found mainly in the northern mountains, especially the Picos de Europa National Park (see box on page 35). Brown bears catch fish and eat berries and roots, and have a life expectancy of about 30 years.

The pardel lynx is also a rare species. Unique to Spain, it is a small type of lynx found mainly in the woodlands of the south and west and in Andalusia's Doñana National Park (see box on page 35). It is light fawn with dark brown spots, and has a short tail and long cheek whiskers, with tufts on the ends of its ears. It feeds on small mammals and birds and is mainly nocturnal (active at night).

Wolves were an endangered species in the recent past, but their numbers are now on the increase. They can be found in the north-west, in much the same territory as the brown bear, and also in the meseta west of Madrid and in western Andalusia. Wolves are protected, but many local people still regard them as enemies.

Birds of prey

Spain has many magnificent birds of prey, some of them rare and found only in remote areas. They are now protected against hunters, and their numbers are gradually increasing. In the high Pyrenees, the lammergeier, or bearded vulture, uses its 2 m (7 ft) wing span to ride the air currents. Its Spanish name is *quebrantahuesos* (bone-breaker), which refers to the way it takes bones from carrion (dead animals) and drops them from a height on to rocks to smash them open and feed on the marrow inside.

The black vulture is another very rare carrion feeder with an even bigger wing span (over 2.5 m/8 ft).

Spain has probably the largest concentration of these birds, although they still number only a few hundred pairs. They can be seen in the Monfragüe Natural Park west of Toledo and in the west of Majorca.

The Spanish imperial eagle is an even more endangered species, mainly found in the forest of the Doñana National Park. It feeds mostly on rabbits and other small mammals and birds.

Spain has many other smaller birds of prey, including kestrels, buzzards, sparrowhawks, red and black kites and, on the Balearic island of Cabrera, Eleonora's falcons.

The Spanish ibex is a sturdy, goat-like creature whose amazing agility enables it to climb almost vertical cliff faces. The males have long, distinctive horns. The Spanish ibex was also threatened with extinction during the 20th century. Following bans on hunting and programmes of captive breeding, ibex numbers have increased rapidly and there are now about 70,000 individuals. Among their habitats are the steep slopes of the Sierra de Gredos in north-central Spain.

More common species

Spain is also home to animals found elsewhere in Europe. Red, roe and fallow deer live in forests and woodlands. Wild boar thrive in thick woodland and marshy areas. The genet, though not rare, is seldom seen because it is nocturnal. It is a spotted, cat-like creature that feeds on small mammals, birds and birds' eggs. Even more common creatures include the squirrel,

Spain's national parks

Since the 1980s, intense efforts have been made to preserve Spain's natural habitat and protect wildlife from the threats created by overgrazing, mining, hydroelectric projects, pesticides and pollution of rivers. There are now twelve national parks, seven in mainland Spain, four in the Canary Islands and one in the Balearics. These are managed by central government; there are hundreds of other protected areas administered by the governments of the autonomous communities.

Spain's first national park was La Montaña de Covadonga in the Picos de Europa, created in 1918. It is home to many rare plants and butterflies, as well as the endangered brown bear.

The Doñana National Park in the Guadalquivir delta is a vital reserve for bird life. Hundreds of thousands winter there, and many migrating birds stop to rest there in spring and autumn.

The Aigüestortes and Sant Maurici Lake National Park in

Catalonia has some of the most spectacular scenery in the Pyrenees, with high peaks, lakes and dramatic waterfalls. There are beech and silver birch forests, with chamois (a goat-sized antelope) and golden eagles on the higher slopes.

The Cabrera Archipelago National Park in the Balearics has rare plants, reptiles and seabirds, and the coastal waters support a rich marine life.

In the Canary Islands, La Palma, Tenerife and Lanzarote each has a national park dedicated to conserving their distinctive volcanic landscapes. La Gomera's national park protects its unique woodland.

There are also parts of the Spanish mainland that are officially reserved for hunting. Here, the wildlife is controlled and managed, and some shooting for sport is permitted.

PICOS DE EUROPA

ORDESA AND MONTE PERDIDO

AIGÜESTORTES AND SANT MAURICI LAKE

CABAÑEROS

TABLAS DE DAIMIEL

CABRERA ARCHIPELAGO

DOÑANA

SIERRA NEVADA

CALDERA DE TABURIENTE

TEIDE

TIMANFAYA

GARAJONAY

badger, fox, otter and pine marten, as well as bats, lizards and snakes. However, some of Spain's great variety of butterflies and moths are unique, as are some of the lizards found on the Balearic Islands.

Gibraltar is claimed by Spain but is a British possession. The Barbary apes of Gibraltar number a few dozen and have a keeper from the British Army to feed and care for them – no doubt because, according to legend, if the apes disappear, the British will be forced to leave the Rock. The Barbary apes are actually macaque monkeys. They are the only wild monkeys in Europe.

Spain's bird species

Spain's rich and diverse bird population includes bustards and capercaillies, quails and partridges, woodpeckers and owls, and white and black storks. The black stork is quite rare and is protected, but the white stork (actually black and white) is more common and can be seen nesting on chimneys and rooftops in the towns of Extremadura.

The deltas of the Guadalquivir and Ebro rivers are

The Barbary macaques of Gibraltar – a British colony off the southern tip of Spain – are the only wild primates in Europe. Legend has it that when the apes disappear from the Rock, so will the British.

great havens for bird life – for wintering ducks and waders, as well as for terns, gulls and flamingos. Seen mostly in the south of Spain, the golden oriole, the hoopoe and the bee-eater are some of the most colourful of the country's birds. The wild serin, a finch native to the Canary Islands, is the species from which domesticated canaries were bred.

MADRID

The Spanish capital, Madrid, is the country's largest city, with a population of nearly 3 million in the city, and 5.1 million with its suburbs. It is the seat of Spain's government and parliament, a thriving business and tourist centre, and the focal point from which roads and railway lines fan out across the land. In one of Madrid's great squares, the Puerta del Sol, a plaque set in the ground is labelled 'Kilometre Zero', marking the point from which all road distances are measured.

The city's history

Madrid has achieved this commanding position only in the last few centuries. Many of Spain's other cities are much older. Madrid, however, had the advantage of a central position in the country. It also had no ties with powerful institutions, such as the Catholic church, which might challenge the power of the government. It is first recorded in the 10th century, when it was a small Moorish town named Majerit. In 1561, King Philip II moved his court to the city, which became the capital in 1607. Philip was the most powerful monarch of his time, obsessed with controlling a vast European and American empire.

As the capital, Madrid attracted large numbers of nobles, churchmen, officials, craftsmen and servants, as well as thieves, beggars and people of all sorts in search of work or patronage. In the following century, these included some of Spain's greatest figures, including the writers Miguel de Cervantes (1547–1616; see box on

Madrid's Plaza Major was built in the early 17th century. The influence of the architect Juan de Herrera, who designed a number of buildings in the city, can be seen in the slate spires.

page 95) and Lope de Vega (1562–1635; see page 96), and the painter Diego Velázquez (1599–1660; see page 99).

Madrid grew rapidly during Spain's Golden Age, which ended in the late 17th century. A period of decline was followed by a partial recovery in the 18th century under a new **dynasty**, the Bourbons. Especially under Charles III (1759–88), new, spacious areas were laid out beyond the crowded old city.

Decline set in again under Charles IV (1788–1808). In 1808, Charles was ousted and Spain came under French control. On 2 May 1808, the people of Madrid rose in revolt against the army of occupation, launching a long war of liberation (see box on page 41). In Spanish, the date of the revolt is called the Dos de Mayo.

The 19th and 20th centuries were turbulent times for Madrid, but it continued to grow. In 1936, after the outbreak of the Spanish Civil War, it was held by the **Republicans** and besieged by the rebel **Nationalists** led by General Franco. The city held out until the three-year

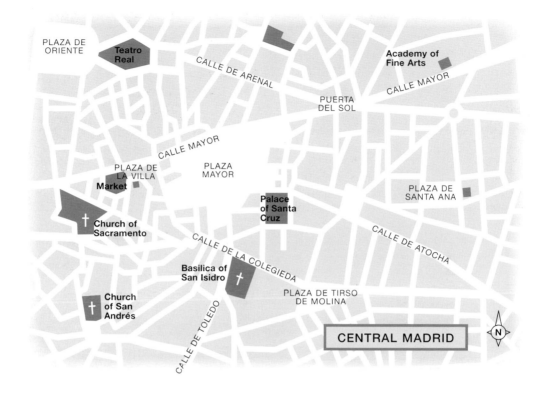

Map labels: PLAZA DE ORIENTE · Teatro Real · CALLE DE ARENAL · Academy of Fine Arts · CALLE MAYOR · PUERTA DEL SOL · CALLE MAYOR · PLAZA DE LA VILLA · Market · PLAZA MAYOR · PLAZA DE SANTA ANA · Church of Sacramento · Palace of Santa Cruz · CALLE DE LA COLEGIEDA · CALLE DE ATOCHA · Basilica of San Isidro · Church of San Andrés · PLAZA DE TIRSO DE MOLINA · CALLE DE TOLEDO · CENTRAL MADRID · N

conflict ended in a Nationalist victory. Though living standards were poor under Franco's dictatorship in the 1940s and 1950s, hundreds of thousands of peasants left the countryside to look for work in Madrid. Many of them lived on the outskirts in shanty towns.

Conditions gradually improved, especially after the death of Franco in 1975 and the restoration of democracy. A new, skyscraper-lined business district grew up along the Paseo de la Castellana, a thoroughfare north of the older centres. Improved amenities made the older centres magnets for Spanish and foreign tourists. Many parts of the city became well known for their vivid street scenes and late-night entertainment and dance clubs.

Madrid's ancient heart lies in a tangle of streets around Plaza Mayor and the Puerta del Sol. The city's major art galleries, including the Prado, mainly stand east of the centre.

The city's landmarks

The old city of Madrid is a relatively small network of irregular streets around three of the city's squares. The Plaza Mayor (Main Square) is a massive, arcaded and

El Escorial

King Philip II made Madrid his capital, but he chose a site outside Madrid, on the slopes of the Sierra Guadarrama, to build a granite structure that was both a monastic royal burial place and a royal palace. Designed by Juan Bautista de Toledo and later by Juan de Herrera, El Escorial, unlike many Spanish buildings, has a plain exterior, which makes its huge bulk seem overpowering. Inside, the grand royal apartments are filled with paintings. Almost all the Spanish monarchs since the 16th century lie in the building in marble coffins.

balconied rectangle built by Philip III in 1617–19. It was formerly used for public displays ranging from bull-fights to public executions. The Puerta del Sol (Gate of the Sun) is one of the city's most popular meeting places, thronged with traffic, sightseers and café patrons. Like Trafalgar Square in London, it attracts crowds of revellers on New Year's Eve. At midnight, it is customary to swallow a grape for good luck as each stroke sounds from the clock tower. The Plaza de la Villa (Municipal Square) is the square with the oldest buildings, notably the 15th-century Torre de los Lujanes (Lujanes' Tower).

Bourbon Madrid lies to the east and west of the old city. To the west, the vast 18th-century Palacio Real (Royal Palace) has 2800 rooms. The area to the east of the old city is closed off by the leafy avenues of the Parque de Retiro, a huge public park that was originally private pleasure grounds built for Philip IV.

Between the old city and the Parque lies 'the golden triangle' – a trio of museums that have made Madrid one of the world's great art centres. The Museo del Prado (Prado Museum) is Spain's long-established national gallery, filled with Spanish masterpieces and many famous works from other countries. The Centro de Arte Reina Sofía (Queen Sofía's Art Centre) has an impressive collection of 20th-century art. Its great showpiece is Spanish artist Pablo Picasso's (1881–1973; see pages 100–1) painting *Guernica*, the artist's response to a Civil War atrocity. The 'triangle' has existed only since 1993, when Spain acquired one of the world's greatest private collections of art, the Thyssen-Bornemisza collection, which is now housed in the Villahermosa Palace.

BARCELONA

Barcelona is a large Mediterranean port on the north-east coast of Spain. The first-known settlement on the site was made by the Romans, who called it Barcino. With a population of about 3.8 million in its metropolitan area, it is Spain's second-largest city. It is also the capital of the autonomous community of Catalonia, and its people generally share the Catalan distrust

May Days

One of the most celebrated episodes in Spanish history is El Dos de Mayo (the Second of May) in 1808, when the people of Madrid rose in revolt against the French. Sporadic attacks on the occupying troops turned into desperate battles at several points in the city where the rebels were concentrated. In the centre, at the Puerta del Sol, a unit of France's Mameluke (Egyptian) cavalry met with fanatical resistance from men and women using any weapon that came to hand. The rising was suppressed, but it marked the beginning of popular resistance to French rule. The Dos de Mayo and the executions of rebels on the following day (El Tres de Mayo) were immortalized in paintings by the Spanish artist Francisco Goya (see page 69).

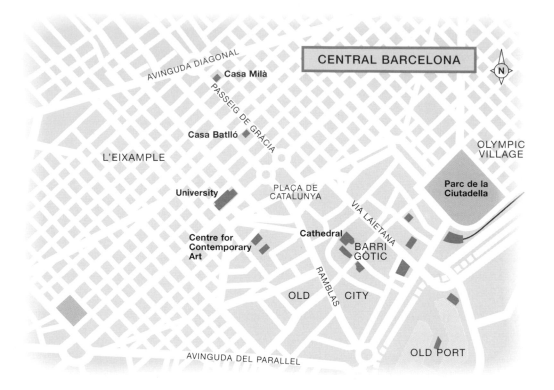

CENTRAL BARCELONA

AVINGUDA DIAGONAL

Casa Milà

PASSEIG DE GRÀCIA

Casa Batlló

L'EIXAMPLE

OLYMPIC
VILLAGE

University

PLAÇA DE
CATALUNYA

Parc de la
Ciutadella

VIA LAIETANA

Centre for
Contemporary
Art

Cathedral

BARRI
GÒTIC

RAMBLAS

OLD   CITY

OLD PORT

AVINGUDA DEL PARALLEL

The small, twisting streets of Barcelona's Old City cluster near the dockside, reflecting the city's historical importance as a port. Newer quarters, such as L'Eixample, follow a more regular grid pattern.

of Madrid and the central government. Since the 1980s, a large-scale programme of redevelopment has made Barcelona a dynamic modern city.

The rise of Barcelona

Barcelona's rise began in the 9th century AD, when it was freed from the Moors and was the centre of the County of Barcelona. A wealthy and self-governing region, it enjoyed a Golden Age during the 13th and 14th centuries. By the late 15th century, when the union of Castile and Aragon created a united Spain, Barcelona was less prosperous. The Catalans twice tried to win their independence by force. As a result, Barcelona was besieged and taken in 1652 and again, very destructively, in 1714.

In the 1940s and 1950s, Barcelona suffered under the dictatorship of the Nationalist leader, General Franco. Following Franco's death in 1975 and the restoration of democracy, Barcelona became the capital of a newly autonomous Catalonia.

The decision to hold the 1992 Olympic Games in the city led to the regeneration of large areas, particularly the waterfront. The Port Vell (Old Port) and the coast to the north-east were transformed into a smart development comprising a marina, apartments, open-air cafés and places of entertainment.

The Old City

Behind the waterfront lies the Ciutat Vella (Old City). At its heart, the Barri Gòtic (**Gothic** Quarter) has many medieval buildings. Most of old Barcelona is built in the medieval Gothic style, with its pinnacles and pointed arches, and the style persisted in Barcelona long after it had been abandoned else-where. Barcelona Cathedral, in the Barri Gòtic, is a medieval building with a 19th-century front in the Gothic style.

Barcelona's famous long avenue, Las Ramblas (see box below), passes beside the Barri Gòtic. Beyond it lies L'Eixample (The Extension), a large area with streets laid out on a grid plan. Built for the newly prosperous 19th-century middle class, it contains most of the building done in Barcelona's extremely fanciful style, called *modernista* (modernist), such as the Casa Batlló designed by Antoni Gaudí (see pages 104 and 105).

South of the old port lies the large green hill of Montjuïc, where there are buildings from several different centuries. The castle dates from 1640, the National Palace was constructed as part of the 1929 World's Fair and the Olympic Stadium dates from 1936. The stadium was refurbished for the 1992 Olympics.

Las Ramblas

Las Ramblas has been called Spain's most famous street. It is a long, straight five-section avenue that runs north-west through the old town to Barcelona's waterfront. It suffered a destructive fire in 1994, and many of the buildings have since been reconstructed. Las Ramblas is filled with cafés and street entertainers. Natives and visitors stroll about and browse among stalls selling everything from books to flowers. Las Ramblas offers a modern equivalent to the centuries-old Mediterranean tradition of informal strolling and self-display.

Barcelona is visited by 3.5 million tourists every year. Its Catalan roots remain strong (as does its rivalry with and suspicion of Madrid). The Catalan government, based in Barcelona, promotes the Catalan language, but both Spanish and Catalan are widely spoken in the city itself, to which as many as 2 million people have immigrated from other parts of Spain since 1940. There are also many immigrants from non-European cultures.

SEVILLE

Seville is the capital of Andalusia and its largest city, with a population of about 1.2 million in the metropolitan area. Its site on the banks of the Guadalquivir River contributes to its greatly admired romantic atmosphere. The river also made Seville a major port,

Seville's cathedral is one of the three largest in the world. Local legend has it that the cathedral builders declared, 'Let us create such a building that future generations will take us for lunatics'.

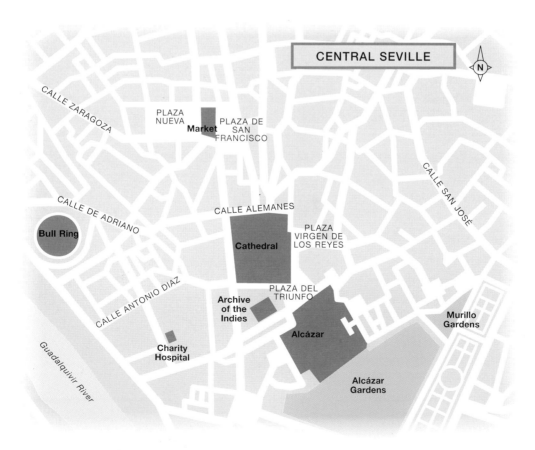

CENTRAL SEVILLE

N

CALLE ZARAGOZA

PLAZA NUEVA
Market
PLAZA DE SAN FRANCISCO

CALLE SAN JOSÉ

CALLE DE ADRIANO

Bull Ring

CALLE ALEMANES

Cathedral

PLAZA VIRGEN DE LOS REYES

CALLE ANTONIO DÍAZ

PLAZA DEL TRIUNFO

Archive of the Indies

Murillo Gardens

Alcázar

Guadalquivir River

Charity Hospital

Alcázar Gardens

situated at the furthest navigable point (100 kilo-metres/60 miles inland).

Seville is famous for colourful public displays, of which the best known is Holy Week (Semana Santa), when processions with religious images are greeted with extremes of joy and grief. Holy Week is quickly followed by the Fería de Abril, a week-long fair which is dedicated to dressing up and lively entertainment.

The city was founded in Roman times, but only achieved prominence in the 11th century AD, when the Moorish **emirate**, dominated by Cordoba, broke up. It became the capital of a prosperous Moorish state stretching across most of Andalusia. In 1248, it was taken by the army of Christian Castile and only slowly recovered from the religious persecution that followed.

Columbus's arrival in the Americas transformed Seville's fortunes. In 1503, the city was granted a monopoly of Spain's transatlantic trade, and for most of the 16th and 17th centuries, it was the wealthiest city in Spain. Famous artists who worked in Seville during this period included Francisco de Zurbarán (1598–1664), Bartolomé Esteban Murillo (1618–82) and Juan de Valdés Leal (1622–90). The great Spanish painter Diego

The Alcázar in Seville was built in the 10th century AD and has been added to over the centuries. The large gardens mostly date from the 16th and 17th centuries, although some were created as recently as the 20th century.

Velázquez (1599– 1660; see page 99) was born in Seville but later left to make a career for himself at the royal court in Madrid.

Surviving monuments from Seville's famous past include the Alcázar (fortress) and the cathedral. Situated very close to each other, they stand in the heart of the old city on the east bank of the river. The Alcázar was a Moorish fortress, added to from the 1360s when a Castilian king, Pedro the Cruel, built a palace for himself inside it. Fortunately Pedro employed **Mudéjar** craftsmen (Moors who continued to live and work under Christian rule). So, despite some later additions, the Alcázar has preserved its Moorish character.

Seville Cathedral is one of the largest churches in the world. It was built over a demolished mosque in a little more than a century (1401–1506), and everything about it is huge and, on the inside, very ornate. The central nave soars to a height of 43 metres (140 feet) and the main altar contains over 1000 carvings.

Next to the cathedral stands La Giralda, a 90-metre (300-foot) belfry tower that was originally a minaret (a tower from which **Muslims** are summoned to prayer). It is one of Seville's great landmarks and has become a symbol of the city.

Seville declined during the 18th century and made only modest progress until recent times. Then came the 1992 Seville Expo, a world's fair in which over 100 countries participated. To host it, the city embarked on an ambitious programme of improvements, including road and bridge-building and the establishment of a high-speed rail link with Madrid. Today, despite its traditional image, Seville is a thoroughly modern city.

BILBAO

With about 950,000 people in the metropolitan area, Bilbao stands on an estuary just inland from Spain's northern coast. It is the country's leading port and the largest Basque city.

Bilbao has a 14th-century riverside quarter, the Casco Viejo, with narrow, winding streets and a Gothic cathedral. It became a major city only in the mid-19th century, however, when iron deposits were discovered nearby and industrialization arrived. Steelworks and chemical factories were set up in Bilbao, and shipbuilding complemented the city's maritime trade.

By the late 20th century, much of Bilbao's heavy industry was disappearing, but it was replaced by new forms of commerce, including a thriving café culture in the Casco Viejo. The adjustment was helped by the construction of Bilbao's most famous building, the Guggenheim Museum (see photograph on page 105). Designed by leading American architect Frank Gehry and opened in 1997, its extraordinary, wavy exterior is sheathed in **titanium**, a rarely used material that creates a brilliant, silvery surface. Inside, the galleries house modern works of art from the collection of the New York Guggenheim Museum and local collections.

The Casco Viejo, Bilbao's historical centre, lies on the right bank of the Bilbao River. The quarters on the left bank date largely from the 19th and 20th centuries.

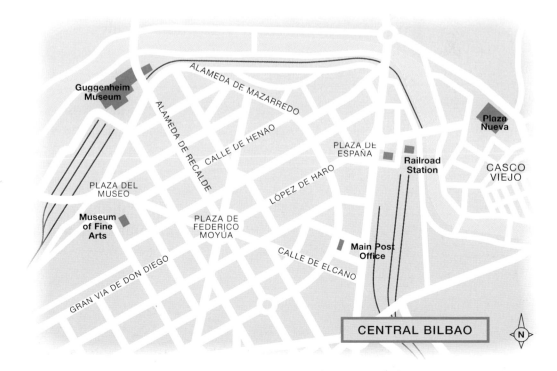

47

Moorish cities

The Moors ruled southern Spain for about eight centuries. Great cities such as Cordoba, Granada and Seville were wealthy and highly civilized. Because the Moors were Muslims, the Christian Spaniards who conquered them destroyed much of their handiwork. But in Cordoba and Granada, magnificent examples of Moorish art and architecture can still be seen today.

Cordoba stands on the Guadalquivir River and grew up in Roman times as a prosperous port. The philosopher Seneca and the poet Lucan were famous Romans from Cordoba. Within a few decades of the Moorish invasion (AD 711), Cordoba became their capital.

After Moorish Spain became independent in 756, the emir, Abdul Rahman I, began to build a great mosque, the Mezquita, which was added to by later rulers. For over two centuries, the city was the largest and wealthiest in Europe, renowned for its huge population, its libraries, public baths and hospitals, and its Moorish and Jewish scholars. Taken by Christian forces in 1236, Cordoba declined in importance. A Christian cathedral was built inside the

The vast Mezquita in Cordoba is situated on the north bank of the Guadalquivir River. The Puente Romano (Roman Bridge), seen here on the right, has been heavily restored.

Water is an important feature of the Generalife gardens and courtyards of the Alhambra palace complex in Granada, creating cool and calm oases in the searing heat.

Mezquita, but the structure survived and is famous for its fantastic decoration and dense horseshoe arches. Cordoba's Alcázar (fortress) and terraced gardens are also notable. Today, with a population of about 310,000, Cordoba is a quiet and relaxed city. Its Moorish traditions live on in the leather and silver craftwork for which it is famous.

Granada's greatest period began later, when Moorish power was waning. It was the capital of the Moorish kingdom that resisted the Reconquest (see page 58) longer than any other, surrendering only in 1492. The fabulous Alhambra, a huge palace and fortress, was begun in the 13th century by Muhammad al-Ghalib, the first of the Nasrid ruling dynasty. The Alhambra and the Generalife gardens above them are set against the spectacular backdrop of the Sierra Nevada. The Court of Lions and other parts of the interior are filled with superb, intricate decoration.

The Alhambra was largely forgotten by the outside world until the publication of *Tales of the Alhambra* in 1832 by the American writer Washington Irving, who also wrote the story 'Rip Van Winkle'.

Past and present

'At a time when even kings could not read or write, a Moorish king had a private library of 600,000 books.'

S. P. Scott in *The History of the Moorish Empire in Europe* (1904)

Spanish history has been turbulent, with dramatic changes of fortune and many wars and civil wars. Among the influences on this history have been religion, regional loyalties and Spain's geographical position, linked with both Europe and Africa, the Atlantic Ocean and the Mediterranean Sea.

In ancient times, settlers and invaders from the Mediterranean brought many new ideas and techniques. Phoenicians, Greeks and Carthaginians were followed by the Romans, who made Spain part of their empire. Even after the Roman empire had fallen its influence lived on in the Latin language, which evolved into Spanish, and in the Christian religion.

Germanic warriors, the Visigoths, replaced the Romans, only to be defeated by **Muslim** invaders from north Africa. Divided between Christian and Muslim states, medieval Spain created a culture in which Christians, Muslims and Jews were able to live and work peacefully together.

A less tolerant but powerful state had emerged by 1492. By coincidence, the country's final unification that year coincided with a Spanish expedition, led by Christopher Columbus, to what Europeans called the 'New World'. Spain acquired a vast colonial empire, and silver and gold from the Americas helped to finance its efforts to dominate Europe. Exhausted by the end of

Toledo was the capital of the kingdom the Visigoths set up in the 6th century AD, and later became the main city of central Muslim Spain.

Altamira

The prehistoric paintings and engravings in the caves at Altamira in Cantabria were discovered in 1879. They demonstrated such skill and were so realistic that for a long time experts did not believe they were genuine. Bison, boars and other creatures were painted accurately and in vivid colours. In some instances, the artist even skilfully incorporated bumps on the cave walls to make the figures seem three-dimensional. Eventually, they were recognized as belonging to the ancient Magdalenian culture. In 1996 new measurements dated the paintings to between 12,800 and 11,100 BC.

the 17th century, Spain fell behind other leading European powers. In the 19th century, the empire was lost, and struggles between social groups intensified.

The Spanish Civil War of 1936–39 became one of the landmark events of the 20th century. It was followed by General Franco's backward-looking dictatorship, which lasted until 1975. Then, astonishingly, there followed a rapid transformation of Spain into a modern, democratic and prosperous country.

SPAIN'S PREHISTORY

Spain was inhabited at a very early date by the remote ancestors of present-day human beings. Bones have been discovered that date back to about 800,000 years ago. Another important find was the 50,000-year-old skull of 'Gibraltar Woman', one of the **Neanderthals**. She was a relative of modern humans (*Homo sapiens sapiens*), who emerged about 10,000 years later.

Modern humans lived during the most recent Ice Age, when glaciers covered much of Europe. Towards its end, between about 20,000 and 8000 BC, a culture named the Magdalenian developed in southern France and northern Spain. The first great works of art in Spain were painted in caves at Altamira, near Santander, about 15,000 to 13,000 years ago (see box opposite).

After the Ice Age ended, new peoples entered Spain. The Iberians probably came from north Africa. They, too, made paintings, in rock shelters. By about 3800 BC, megalithic (large stone) tombs were being put up around the Spanish coast. Farming followed about 1300 years later, along with copper-working. By about 2000 BC, the Bronze Age had begun in Spain.

From about 1000 BC, more newcomers, the Celts, arrived from the north, bringing with them ironworking techniques. In central Spain, the two groups mixed, and the people there are known as Celtiberians.

Ancient invaders

By 1200 BC, the Mediterranean coast of Spain was being visited by the Phoenicians. They were maritime traders who were originally from Syria and Lebanon. In the 9th century BC or earlier, they founded the city of Gadir, which became the modern city of Cadiz. Even more important, they brought a Phoenician invention, the alphabet, with them which the Iberians then adapted to create their first writing system.

The Phoenicians traded their wine and oil for Spanish silver. By about 600 BC, they had rivals in the Greeks, who had set up colonies all over the eastern Mediterranean and were seeking to move into the west. As well as goods for trade, the Greeks introduced the potter's wheel and a recent invention – money. Around 575 BC, Greeks from the colony at Marseille, on the French coast, established Emporion (Greek for 'market place') in Spain.

Helped by these contacts with the Greeks, the Iberians developed a more advanced culture, living in large hilltop towns. They became skilful artists, producing pottery and stone sculptures, including the well-known *Lady of Elche*.

The Lady of Elche, as this sculpture is known, was made in about the 5th century BC. It was excavated from the town of Elche in Valencia.

RULE BY CARTHAGE AND ROME

Late in the 6th century BC, the Greeks were displaced by the Carthaginians, a people of Phoenician origin who had created a commercial empire in the western Mediterranean. Carthaginian ambitions in Spain were limited until the mid-3rd century BC, when they were driven from Sicily by the rising power of Rome and looked for compensation in Iberia. Despite fierce resistance, they conquered the southern and central regions, making the east coast city of Novo Cartago (modern Cartagena in Murcia) their capital.

The Romans also advanced into the peninsula and took control of the north-east coast. In 218 BC, Rome sought to prevent Carthage obtaining military reinforcements from Spain. The dispute led to the Second Punic (Carthaginian) War, which ended in 202 BC with a decisive Roman victory. Spain itself was conquered between 211 and 207 BC and became part of the rapidly growing

Roman empire. The expansion of Roman power was slow, for the Iberian tribes of the interior resisted fiercely. The conquest of the peninsula was only completed in AD 19, when a Roman general, Agrippa, occupied Cantabria in the far north.

Large-scale settlement by Romans began in the late first century BC, and the Roman way of life was gradually adopted by the peoples of Hispania (the Roman word from which 'España', the Spanish word for 'Spain', is derived). Cities were furnished with public buildings, baths, **aqueducts** and other amenities, and villas appeared in the countryside. Most of the native languages were replaced by Latin, the language of the Romans. Spain prospered, exporting olive oil, grain, wool, metals and *garum*, a potent, immensely popular fish sauce. During the fourth century AD, Spain, like the rest of the empire, became officially Christian.

Spanish Romans

Spaniards played significant roles in Roman history. Two of them, Trajan and Hadrian, were among the 'five good emperors' who ruled during the 2nd century AD, when the empire was most powerful and secure. And it was a Spanish emperor, Theodosius the Great, who in 392 completed the triumph of Christianity by ordering the complete suppression of the old **pagan** religions. The Roman poets Martial and Lucan were born in Spain, and so was the philosopher and statesman Seneca.

VISIGOTHS AND MOORS

Roman Spain shared the misfortunes of the empire as it struggled to cope with raids and invasions by 'barbarian' Germanic tribes. During the 3rd century AD, huge walls were built to protect Spanish towns. The empire recovered for a time, but in the 5th century, things began to fall apart. Barbarians broke into the empire at several places, and Spain was occupied many times. Eventually, in 507, a Germanic people, the Visigoths, set up a longer-lived kingdom with its capital at Toledo.

The Visigoths formed a relatively small warrior **elite**. The majority of the population were Roman civilians whose Latin speech was already beginning to evolve

Toledo was an important city on the Iberian peninsula in Roman times. The Roman name for it was Toletum. Today, it is still known as La Cuidad Imperial (The Imperial City).

into Spanish. Differences between the Visigoths and the majority gradually disappeared, and there was a limited cultural revival led by bishop-scholars such as Isidore of Seville (*c*.560–636). However, the security of the kingdom was constantly undermined by feuds within the royal family and aristocratic plots and revolts. Finally, in 710, a civil war broke out just when a formidable foe was ready to strike.

The invaders were Arabs and Berbers, often known as **Moors**, who in 711 crossed over to Gibraltar from north Africa. In fact, Gibraltar is named after one of the Arab generals: it comes from Jabal Tariq, Arabic for 'the Mountain of Tariq'. The Moors brought with them the new religion of **Islam**.

The Moorish army rapidly overran Spain, and the last Visigothic king of Spain was drowned while fleeing after a battle. The Moors pushed on over the Pyrenees

The Mezquita (Great Mosque) of Cordoba was founded in AD 785. It was extended over the following centuries, and a cathedral was built in the middle of it in the 16th century.

into France, but they were turned back in 732 at the Battle of Poitiers. Their armies never advanced so far north again. Meanwhile, Spanish Christians held out in Asturias in the north-west and in the Basque Country.

At first, disputes between Arabs and Berbers seemed likely to destabilize Muslim Spain – known as al Andalus. Then, in 756, Abd al Rahman arrived. He was the last survivor of the Ummayad **dynasty**, which had ruled the entire Islamic world until its overthrow in 750. Abd al Rahman subdued all the rival groups and made al Andalus an independent **emirate** with its capital at Cordoba. One of his successors, Abd al Rahman III, went further and, in 929, declared himself and his successors **caliphs** – political and religious rulers.

Many Christians converted to Islam, and those who remained Christians commonly adopted Arab culture and language. They formed a distinctive group, known as Mozarabs.

A flourishing Islamic state

The early centuries were the great age of al Andalus. During this period, Islamic civilization was more advanced than that of Christian Europe. Arab culture had absorbed Greek science and philosophy and Hindu mathematics, which were hardly known in Christian Europe until much later.

Efficient agriculture and foreign trade made the country rich and populous, scholarship flourished and the magnificent buildings of Cordoba made it the most splendid city in Europe. Communities of Muslims, Christians and Jews lived side by side, since Islam was relatively tolerant. The main burden borne by non-Muslims was extra taxation. Jewish communities flourished in medieval Spain, producing poets and great philosophers such as Moses Maimonides (1135–1204).

The last great leader of the Ummayad caliphate was Al Mansur, chief minister from 981 to 1002. After his death, the caliphate declined. Rival factions fought civil wars, and in 1031, a revolt in Cordoba overthrew the caliphate. Islamic Spain broke up into a number of small states, or *taifas*, and their lack of unity allowed the Christian states of the north to gain the upper hand.

THE RECONQUEST

Military advances by these states eventually united Spain under Christian rule. This centuries-long process is usually described as the Reconquest, although it often lapsed when Christian states fought one another or made alliances with the Muslim *taifas*.

By the early 11th century, five Christian states had emerged in the north and had managed to enlarge their territories: the kingdoms of León, Castile, Navarre and Aragon, plus the county of Barcelona. During the 11th century, Castile became the dominant Christian power, pressing forward into central Spain. In 1085, King Alfonso VI's army captured the former Visigothic capital, Toledo, the first important setback for the Moors.

The *taifas* were weakened by their disunity, and most of them paid tribute to one or other of the Christian states. However, both sides were fairly tolerant during this period, and alliances were often made between Muslims and Christians.

The situation began to change towards the end of the 11th century. The *taifas* were alarmed by Alfonso VI's victories and appealed for help to the Almoravids, a militant Muslim **sect** that had just conquered Morocco in north Africa. The Almoravids crossed into Spain and in 1086 inflicted a crushing defeat on Alfonso, who did, however, hold on to Toledo. The Almoravids rapidly united Moorish Spain, taking a far less tolerant attitude towards non-Muslims. In the 1140s, the Almoravids had lost much of their strength, but they were replaced by an equally intolerant north African sect, the Almohads.

The Moors begin to lose their grip

The Christian kingdoms of Castile and Aragon were strengthened by unions with their neighbours. In 1137, Aragon and the county of Barcelona were united, and in 1230, Castile and León followed suit. A turning point in the war against the Moors came in July 1212, when a combined Christian force shattered the Almohads at

As the Muslim rulers of Spain became less tolerant of other religions from the end of the 11th century onwards, a similar ebbing of tolerance occurred among Christians. They were influenced by the religious fervour that was sweeping Europe, which came to a head in the First Crusade of 1096.

Las Navas de Tolosa. This was followed by decisive advances between 1229 and 1248. Under Ferdinand III, Castilian troops drove south and south-east, capturing Cordoba (1236) and Seville (1248). Castile was now by far the largest and most populous kingdom. But Aragon was advancing as well. The Aragonese, under James 1 also seized the Balearic islands of Majorca and Minorca (1229) and pushed south on the mainland to occupy Valencia (1238). The Portuguese were also active, conquering the last of what became their national territory, the Algarve in the south of the country.

Santiago de Compostela

In AD 813 a tomb was discovered in Galicia that Christians came to believe was the burial place of one of the Christian apostles, James, son of Zebedee (St James the Great). James was martyred in Jerusalem in about AD 44. There was a Spanish tradition that his bones had been buried in Spain, where he had earlier worked as an evangelist. The belief that their soil held such an important shrine greatly strengthened Spanish morale in the struggle against the Moors. A church was built over the shrine, and the town of Santiago de Compostela grew up around it ('Santiago' is Spanish for 'St James'). It soon became a place of pilgrimage for Christians from other parts of western Europe. During the **Middle Ages**, only Rome and Jerusalem were more venerated.

The only surviving Moorish state was the relatively small kingdom of Granada in the far south. It survived for another 250 years, while the Christian kingdoms were distracted by civil wars and exploits outside the peninsula.

Revolts and civil wars plagued Castile, where the nobility had gained huge estates and great privileges. There were also ferocious wars between rival claimants to the throne, notably the long duel (1350–69) between Pedro the Cruel and his half-brother, Henry of Trastamara. French and English armies took a hand before Pedro was defeated and killed in 1369.

Henry managed to establish his dynasty in Castile, and one of his grandsons became king of Aragon in 1412. The two most important Spanish states were now ruled by members of the same family and usually remained on good terms.

El Cid

El Cid is Spain's great legendary hero, who was celebrated for his role in the Christian campaigns to reconquer Spain from the Moors. Although El Cid was a real historical figure, his career was very different from the legend.

He was a Castilian nobleman, born in about 1043, and his name was Rodrigo Diáz de Vivar. 'El Cid' is a Spanish version of the Arabic *sayyid*, meaning 'lord'. El Cid was an outstandingly successful general, but he fell out of favour with the king and went into exile in 1081. Far from fighting the Moors, he fought for the Muslim ruler of Zaragoza.

El Cid gradually increased his influence over another Muslim state, Valencia, captured it in 1094 and remained an independent ruler until his death in 1099.

A few years later, when Valencia fell under Muslim rule again, El Cid's body was transferred to a monastery in Castile. He was already a legendary figure, and his tomb became a shrine. His fame was sealed by Spain's greatest epic poem, the 12th-century *Cantar del mío Cid*.

This illustration depicts El Cid after battle in an illuminated manuscript from the 14th-century.

Aragon's ambitions lay beyond Spain. Possession of the Balearic Islands was followed by Sicily (1282) and Sardinia (1327). The kingdom of Naples (in southern Italy) was effectively acquired in 1442. Though it changed hands several times, in the 16th century, Naples was to become a long-term Spanish possession.

Expanding into the Mediterranean, the Aragonese empire became a formidable trading power. Trade, a vigorous middle class, towns and the kingdom's three parliaments (of Aragon, Catalonia and Valencia) made Aragon very different from Castile. Castilian kings struggled to assert their authority, and the economy was centred around agriculture and sheep-rearing.

THE UNIFICATION OF SPAIN

After the death of Henry IV in 1474, his half-sister, Isabella, took the throne. She was married to Ferdinand, the heir to the Aragonese throne. When Ferdinand came to his throne in 1479, Castile and Aragon were in effect jointly ruled by Ferdinand and Isabella. The two kingdoms kept their own institutions and identities, but people increasingly spoke and thought of Spain as a single country. The monarchy was further strengthened by the final taming of the Castilian nobility.

These developments released Spanish energies, and in 1481, war was resumed against the Moorish kingdom of Granada. One city after another surrendered, and at last, on 2 January 1492, Granada itself gave in.

The Reconquest was complete, but Spanish religious zeal remained unquenched. In 1478, Ferdinand and Isabella had persuaded the pope to establish the Spanish Inquisition, an organization dedicated to rooting out **heresy**. Its main targets were Jews and Muslims who had converted to Christianity; they were suspected of practising their original faith secretly.

Under Spain's first Grand Inquisitor, Tomás de Torquemada, some 2000 people were burnt to death. The unconverted were also persecuted. In March 1492,

During the 14th century, Christians became more intolerant of minorities. Muslim workers were treated more and more badly. Jews were blamed for events such as the Black Death, a plague that swept across Europe in 1348. In 1391, a massacre of Jews in Seville spread into other parts of Spain.

When Jews and Muslims were forced to leave Spain if they did not convert to Christianity, Spain lost many of its most skilled and industrious people – all for the sake of religious unity.

the Jews of Spain were told that they must become Christians or leave the country. Many did convert, but perhaps as many as 200,000 of them left their homeland for good. In 1502, the Moors under Spanish rule were offered the same choice. Those who remained were often persecuted by the Inquisition, and eventually all the Moriscos (converts from Islam) were expelled from Spain. Even after this, the Inquisition retained an extraordinary centuries-long control over Spanish life.

Another great event of 1492 was the European discovery of the Americas by a Spanish expedition led by a Genoese sea captain, Christopher Columbus (see box).

Christopher Columbus

Columbus (1451–1506) was not a Spaniard, but he commanded a Spanish expedition that made the New World known to Europeans.

Born Cristoforo Colombo in the Italian republic of Genoa, Columbus was an experienced seaman and merchant. He became convinced that it was possible to reach India and China by a relatively short westward journey, gaining access to the riches of the East. Failing to convince the king of Portugal, he went to Spain in 1485. After seven years of waiting, Ferdinand and Isabella financed an expedition by three small ships, the *Santa María*, the *Niña* and the *Pinta*.

On 12 October 1492, five weeks after leaving the Canaries, the expedition made landfall on an island Columbus named San Salvador. Further discoveries followed before he returned to Spain with a party of 'Indians' to prove that he had visited 'the Indies'. Columbus made three more expeditions before his death. He landed on the coast of South America, but it is possible that he never realized he had found a New World rather than the old East.

Spain's American empire

Soon after Columbus discovered the New World, Spanish settlers and adventurers took most of the Caribbean islands. The American mainland was explored by men such as Juan Ponce de León, who discovered Florida, and Vasco Nuñez de Balboa, who crossed Panama and sighted the Pacific Ocean.

Small forces of gold-hungry Spaniards used audacity and ruthlessness to defeat the native peoples they encountered.

Hernán Cortés made alliances with local peoples to overthrow the mighty Aztec empire in Mexico (1519–22). Francisco Pizarro subdued the **Incas** of South America (1531–35). The illustration below is from an Aztec manuscript depicting the Spanish and their allies – shown here on horseback – fighting the **Aztecs** in 1519.

Bad treatment and European diseases wiped out huge numbers of the native population. To maintain the labour force, the Spanish shipped black Africans across the Atlantic as slaves. Precious metals flowed back to Spain, especially after the opening of the South American Potosí silver mines in 1545.

By about 1600, Spain possessed an empire that (apart from Portuguese Brazil) stretched from the southern USA south to Argentina.

The Spanish discovery of the Americas had a limited effect at first, but eventually it brought Spain an empire and vast wealth.

Queen Isabella died in 1504, but Ferdinand lived to see Navarre annexed to Castile in 1512. The entire peninsula, with the exception of Portugal, now belonged to the Spanish Crown.

IMPERIAL SPAIN

In 1516, Ferdinand's fifteen-year-old grandson took his place, as Charles I, founding Spain's Habsburg dynasty. Charles benefited from complicated family alliances that gave him a vast European inheritance. Despite an unpromising start, Charles won over the Spanish, and Spanish revenues were vital in enabling him to finance his wars. Less than half his reign was spent in the peninsula, but the Spanish supported him in his conflicts with France, his defence of Catholicism against the new Protestantism in Germany and his campaigns against the Turks advancing into south-east Europe and along the Mediterranean. South-east Europe was far away, but Spaniards had long hoped to conquer north Africa and strongly supported Charles's expeditions against Muslim strongholds in the region. Tunis was captured in 1535, but a second major effort – against Algiers in 1541 – was less successful.

Charles held his empire together until, worn out, he abdicated (gave up his throne). Having realized that the Habsburg dominions were too far-flung for one man to rule effectively, Charles divided them. In 1535 his brother Ferdinand took over Charles's central and east European possessions. In 1556, when Charles abdicated the Spanish throne, his son Philip inherited almost everything else – Spain and Spanish America, much of Italy and the wealthy Netherlands.

Spain was now unmistakably the heart of the empire. Philip II had been brought up as a Spaniard and ruled his realms from the previously unimportant town of Madrid in the centre of the country.

Spain's Golden Age

The 16th and early 17th centuries are often called the Siglio de 'Oro (Golden Age) of Spain. Throughout this time, Spanish culture flourished, and dozens of important writers, artists and religious leaders were active. Politically, the reign of Philip II (1556–98) was its high point.

Philip II rarely left his monastery-palace, the Escorial (see box on page 40). Instead of travelling like his father, he attempted to control his empire by personally reading a never-ending stream of reports and issuing written instructions.

This miniature, dated 1583, shows King Philip II. It was made by the French-born artist Isaac Oliver (c. 1556–1617), who painted many members of European royalty.

Spain was the greatest power in Europe and deeply involved in the bitter struggles taking place on the continent. Spanish armies proved themselves the finest in Europe, but apart from its fighting men, Spain had few resources: Castile was a poor country and Aragon's trade had long passed its peak. Spanish conquests in the New World brought spectacular rewards, however, including huge quantities of silver shipped across the Atlantic from South American mines.

In 1580, Philip was able to claim the Portuguese throne, acquiring a second empire and a second fleet. He was now at the height of his power, directly challenged only by a rebellion in the Netherlands. He also suffered several reversals of fortune, however. The most spectacular of these was the fate of the Spanish Armada, the great fleet sent against England in 1588. Battered and dispersed by the English warships, the Spanish fled northwards and round the British Isles, suffering terrible losses from storms and rocks before a remnant managed to limp back to Spain.

Despite these setbacks, Spain was still formidable under Philip's successors, Philip III (1598–1621) and Philip IV (1621–65). Further European wars sapped its strength, however. Despite long and immensely costly efforts, the Spanish failed to subdue the rebel Dutch **Republic**, which was rapidly becoming a front-rank naval and commercial nation. Meanwhile, in 1622, Spain was also drawn into hostilities with a reunited France. The Spanish fought well, but the war gradually turned against them. In 1628, the Dutch captured the entire fleet bringing the year's treasure from America, and in 1639, they established their naval supremacy at the Battle of the Downs. In 1643, the French destroyed an invading Spanish army at Rocroi, ending Spain's military dominance in Europe.

Meanwhile Spain's chief minister, Count Olivares, tried to create a more centralized form of government.

Spanish forces took part in numerous conflicts during the reign of Philip II. In the Mediterranean, the Spaniards and their Venetian allies won a famous victory over the Turks in 1570 at the naval Battle of Lepanto, depicted here. The Turks quickly recovered, however, and the Spanish advantage was lost.

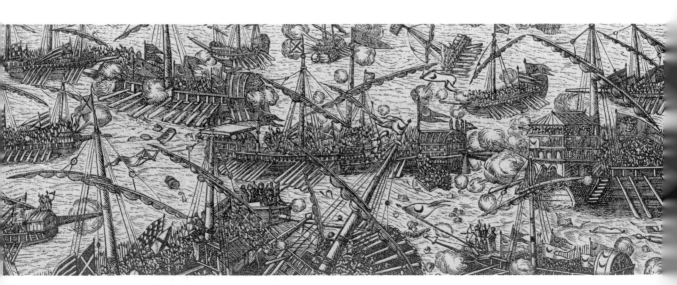

His policies angered the regions, and in 1640, Portugal and Catalonia rose in revolt, followed in 1647 by Naples. Portugal was lost for good, and between 1648 and 1659, Spain was forced to recognize the Dutch Republic and give up fortresses and Pyrenean provinces to France. Catalonia and Naples were subdued and other breakaway attempts were foiled. Badly battered, Spain had at least survived intact.

A change of dynasty

In 1665, a child in poor health, Charles II, came to the throne. He produced no direct heirs, and the future of Spain and its empire after Charles's death became a matter of concern. The leading European states tried to settle the matter by secret treaties that divided up the empire, but Charles was determined to keep it together. When he died in 1700, he left Spain and the empire to Philip, the grandson of King Louis XIV of France – on condition that the inheritance was not split up.

This meant that a member of the French Bourbon dynasty would rule an undivided Spanish empire in place of the Habsburgs. The Austrian Habsburgs, Britain and the Dutch Republic were prepared to fight to prevent such a concentration of power in Bourbon hands. But Louis XIV, the most powerful monarch in Europe, decided to take the risk and accept the inheritance on behalf of his grandson. The long War of the

The Habsburgs

The Habsburgs were German nobles who acquired large landholdings in the 13th century, eventually becoming archdukes of Austria. From 1273, a Habsburg was almost always elected Holy Roman emperor, a position of great prestige but limited power in central Europe. In 1516, marriage alliances brought a Habsburg to the Spanish throne as Charles I. Already the ruler of Burgundy and the Netherlands, he inherited Austria and the German Habsburg lands in 1519, and shortly afterwards was elected Holy Roman emperor as Charles V. Outside Spain, he is best known by this title. With the Spanish possessions in Italy and the Spanish American colonies, Charles ruled a vast empire that he divided before abdicating in 1556. The Spanish Habsburgs died out in 1700, but the Austrian line ruled as emperors until 1918.

Spanish Succession (1701–14) was fought in many parts of Europe, and France, faced by an alliance of enemies, was lucky to survive. In Spain, Louis' grandson became Philip V (1700–46) but had to fight hard to establish himself. Catalonia recognized his Habsburg rival and resisted stubbornly until 1714.

Despite Charles II's wishes, Spain gave up territory as part of the general peace settlement. Losses included a small but strategically very important piece of Spanish soil, Gibraltar, taken by the British. Austria received the Spanish Netherlands (the southern provinces of the Netherlands, which Spain had held against the rebellious Dutch). Some of Spain's other territories, including most of its Italian possessions, had to be given up but were recovered within a few years. It was agreed that the thrones of France and Spain would always be occupied by different members of the Bourbon family.

A REVOLUTIONARY ERA

The French Revolution, which began in 1789, had a powerful impact on Spanish and European politics. France became a republic and its Bourbon king, Louis XVI, was executed. Spain joined other powers in declaring war on France, but French victories forced the Spanish to reverse their policy. Consequently, in 1805, as allies of France's new emperor, Napoleon Bonaparte, Spain's navy shared the fate of the French fleet at the Battle of Trafalgar, an overwhelming victory won by the British admiral Horatio Nelson.

Napoleon remained supreme on land, and in 1807, French and Spanish forces jointly occupied Portugal. The presence of French troops in Spain led to popular protest and quarrels within the royal family, however. Eventually, Napoleon made both Charles IV (reigned 1788–1808) and his son Ferdinand abdicate. Napoleon then appointed his older brother, Joseph, king of Spain.

The news sparked off a revolt by the people in support of the exiled Ferdinand. The French army put down all open resistance, but the Spanish waged a savage guerrilla war. A British army came to their assistance, commanded by Sir Arthur Wellesley, later the Duke of Wellington. The French were driven out in 1813, and Napoleon's empire collapsed soon afterwards.

Although the Spanish had reacted ferociously to foreign rule, the ideas associated with the French invaders had an impact. Among them were the **sovereignty** of the people or nation, expressed through a Constitution and some kind of parliament, along with equality before the law and religious tolerance. The new ideas appealed to the middle class and some people in the army, who came to be known as liberals. They were bitterly opposed by conservatives who upheld the traditional order and were dominated by the monarchy and nobility, as well as by a Church with vast properties and great power over people's lives. The conflict between conservatives and liberals went on all through the 19th and into the 20th centuries.

On 2 May 1808, the people of Madrid rose in revolt against the French, marking the beginning of resistance to French rule. The rebels were executed the following day, an event that was captured in this painting by Francisco Goya (see pages 99–101).

Spain in upheaval

In 1814, Ferdinand returned to Spain and began his reign as Ferdinand VII (1814–33). Now deeply conservative, he rejected a Spanish Constitution drawn up in 1812 and restored the authority of the Inquisition. His reactionary (anti-progressive) policies led to a revolt in 1820, and Ferdinand was forced to accept the Constitution. In 1823, a military intervention by France (where the Bourbons were back on the throne) restored his absolute authority.

After Ferdinand's death, his infant daughter Isabella succeeded to the throne. She was challenged by her uncle, Don Carlos, whose followers were known as Carlists. Spanning several generations, Carlist wars divided Spain on several occasions during the 19th century. At other times, hostility between liberals and conservatives led to a *pronunciamiento* – the seizure of power by a general. During this period of upheaval, Spain briefly became a republic.

Meanwhile, there were revolts in Spain's American empire, most of which was lost. Industrialization was beginning to transform parts of western Europe, but Spain failed to keep up. In Castile, which dominated the country politically, agriculture was unproductive and the people were poverty stricken. Industry grew most in regions that tended to be most hostile to control by Madrid – in Catalonia and in the Basque country.

Increased Stability

The political situation became more stable after a new Constitution was introduced in 1876. In 1890, the right to vote was extended to all men over 24 (but not to women, in Spain or anywhere else in Europe). In practice, however, a wealthy and powerful elite, supported by a conservative Church, was able to control elections all through the 19th century. Discontent continued to simmer, and the reputation of the ruling class took a further blow during the disastrous Spanish-American

The Spanish-American War

From 1895, savage fighting took place between rebels in Cuba (a Spanish island colony in the Caribbean) and Spanish government forces. American public opinion strongly favoured the rebels. Then, on 15 February 1898, the US battleship *Maine* was blown up in the harbour at Havana, the Cuban capital. An investigation named a mine or torpedo as the cause, and although there was no evidence that the Spanish were to blame, war fever rose high in the USA. 'Remember the *Maine*! To hell with Spain!' became a popular slogan. US President McKinley put forward demands that would have led to Cuban independence, and when Spain rejected some of them, war broke out.

The USA easily defeated the ageing Spanish fleet. The photograph below shows the wreck of the Spanish cruiser the *Oquendo*, which was destroyed – along with its sister ships the *Vizcaya* and the *Infanta Maria Teresa* – by US forces in the naval Battle of Santiago, in Cuban waters. The victorious USA then invaded Cuba and the Philippines. When peace was made, the USA acquired the Spanish colonies of the Philippines, Puerto Rico and Guam, and a US administration began steering Cuba towards independence.

War of 1898 (see box on page 71). At the same time, terrorist acts by anarchists and harsh counter-measures intensified, reaching a climax in 1909, when dozens of churches were destroyed and hundreds of workers were executed during 'Tragic Week' in Barcelona.

THE 20TH CENTURY

During the early 20th century, Spain became increasingly divided between the right and the left. The right was composed of deeply conservative forces, such as the aristocracy and the Church, that were identified with wealth and privilege. The left included some republicans and liberals, and groups that stood for more radical change, such as **socialists**, **communists** and **anarchists**.

The right triumphed in 1923, when General Primo de Rivera launched a *pronunciamiento* and established a dictatorship. Unwisely, King Alfonso XIII failed to oppose Primo, and the monarchy shared the dictator's unpopularity. After Primo stepped down in 1930, elections returned an overwhelming republican majority, and Alfonso was forced into exile.

When the first national elections followed in June 1931, an alliance of republicans and socialists won with a huge majority. A new Constitution allowed women to vote in elections for the first time and gave citizens various rights, including complete religious freedom. The Church no longer had a role in politics and lost many of its privileges. Another long-standing grievance was tackled when autonomy (self-government) was granted to Catalonia.

Enthusiasm for the new regime soon cooled. Change was hard to introduce against powerful opposition, and impatience led to violence. Parts of Spain reacted by swinging to the right, which won the 1933 elections. The new government acted brutally towards opposition from Catalans and Asturian miners, and many socialist leaders were arrested. It seemed as though the right was aiming to suppress the republic and end **democracy**.

The threat united the left, which formed a **coalition**, the Popular Front. In the elections of 1936, it won a decisive victory and began a policy of social reform that involved breaking up great estates and giving land to the peasants. In some areas, poor people took direct action and occupied land.

The Spanish Civil War

These developments, along with new restrictions on the Church, horrified the right. Crisis point was reached on 18 July 1936, when an army revolt broke out at Melilla in north Africa and was followed by army uprisings on the mainland. Parts of Spain were occupied by the rebels, but elsewhere loyal troops or **militias** held on for the government. The rebels airlifted over large numbers of troops from north Africa, and a full-scale war began.

The Spanish Civil War became one of the most famous conflicts of the 20th century. The government forces were known as Republicans or Loyalists, the

Troops of Franco's bodyguard march through a street in Madrid after the Nationalist victory in the Spanish Civil War.

The most celebrated unit in the Spanish Civil War was the International Brigade, which fought on the Republican side and suffered heavy casualties.

rebels as **Nationalists** or Insurgents. General Francisco Franco soon emerged as the supreme commander of the Nationalists, and under his leadership the parties of the right were merged into a single National Movement.

Italy and Germany helped the Nationalists and sent their own troops to fight on the Nationalist side. Italy was led by Benito Mussolini and Nazi Germany by Adolf Hitler. They represented a new 20th-century trend generally described as **fascism**. Fascist states were openly anti-democratic and ruled by a single party.

Opposition to fascism made the Spanish Civil War an international issue. Most democratic states remained neutral, but thousands of people left for Spain to fight or help, most of whom sided with the Republicans. The only official help for the Republicans came from the Soviet Union, then the world's only communist state.

The war was bitterly fought, with atrocities committed on both sides. Barcelona fell to the Nationalists in January 1939, and with the later surrender of Madrid and Valencia, the war ended on 1 April. Some 750,000 people may have died, and hundreds of thousands went into exile rather than live under Franco.

Franco's Spain

Franco's Spain was a dictatorship in which no opposition was allowed. There was no free press, and the only 'parliament' was filled with representatives appointed by the government. Strikes were banned, regional rights were abolished and Spanish became the only permitted language. Economic policy was based on close state control and was aimed at making Spain self-sufficient – independent of trade with other countries.

The Civil War was soon followed by World War Two (1939–45). Although officially Spain was neutral, Franco's sympathies were with Hitler and Mussolini.

Spain remained backward and impoverished. Then, in the late 1950s, Franco finally began to allow greater economic freedom and encourage foreign investment.

Businesses hurried to invest in a country where wages were low compared to much of Europe, and the low cost of living attracted many tourists.

Democratic Spain

By the time Franco died in 1975, Spain had modernized economically but remained a dictatorship. Alfonso XIII's grandson, Juan Carlos, inherited the throne and encouraged a return to democracy. In 1976, a moderate politician, Adolfo Suárez, became prime minister. Under Suárez political parties were legalized, democratic elections were held and in 1978, a democratic Constitution was introduced. The first grants of autonomy – to Catalonia and the Basque Country, both traditionally fiercely independent – followed.

Spain took its place as a European power, joining the **North Atlantic Treaty Organization** (NATO) in 1982 and becoming a member of the European Economic Community (now the **European Union** or EU) in 1986.

Franco was a fascist leader like Mussolini and Hitler, although he was more traditional and religious in outlook. Thousands of people were executed during the early months of his regime, in an attempt to 'purify' Spain.

The strength of the new democracy was shown by the way in which changes of government between right and left took place peacefully on the basis of election results. However, violence remains a problem because of the murders and kidnappings carried out by **ETA**, a group determined to secure complete Basque independence. The great majority of Spaniards, including many Basques, are outraged by ETA terrorism.

SPAIN'S ADMINISTRATION

Spain is a constitutional monarchy. The head of state is the monarch (king or queen), who inherits the position. As in the UK, the role of the monarch is mainly ceremonial. The most powerful political figure is the president of the government, or prime minister, who is normally the elected leader of the largest party (or coalition of parties) in the Spanish parliament. The prime minister chooses the Council of Ministers (Cabinet), which decides overall policies.

The Spanish parliament, the Cortes Generales, consists of two houses: the Senate, or upper house, and the Congress of Deputies, or lower house. The Senate

The Spanish national parliament (Cortes Generales) has two houses – the Senate (Senado), or upper house, and Congress of Deputies (Congreso de los Diputados), or lower house. In 1978, considerable power was devolved to the nineteen autonomous communities, which each has its own parliament.

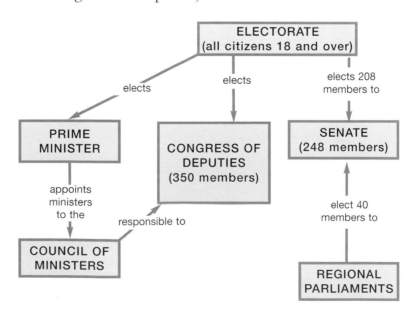

THE SPANISH PARLIAMENT IN 2003

Head of state: King Juan Carlos

Head of government: President José Maria Aznar Lopez

Senate
248 seats • last election 2000 • elections held every four years

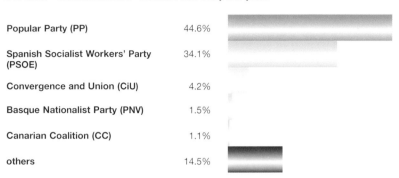

Popular Party (PP)	44.6%
Spanish Socialist Workers' Party (PSOE)	34.1%
Convergence and Union (CiU)	4.2%
Basque Nationalist Party (PNV)	1.5%
Canarian Coalition (CC)	1.1%
others	14.5%

Congress of Deputies
350 seats • last election 2000 • elections held every four years

Popular Party (PP)	44.5%
Spanish Socialist Workers' Party (PSOE)	34%
United Left (IU)	5.4%
Convergence and Union (CiU)	4.2%
Basque Nationalist Party (PNV)	1.5%
Galician Nationalist Bloc (BNG)	1.3%
Canarian Coalition (CC)	1%
others	8.1%

Since 1982, Spanish politics has been dominated by two parties. The Popular Party (PP) encourages the role of private business, whereas the Socialists (PSOE) favour a larger role for the government in regulating the economy.

consists of 208 directly elected members, plus 40 regional representatives elected by the regional parliaments. The Congress of Deputies is the main source of national political power. It is composed of 350 directly elected deputies; elections are held every four years.

The seventeen autonomous regions all have their own parliament and considerable powers of self-government. Spain is also subdivided for administrative purposes into 50 provinces, and Spaniards vote in municipal as well as European parliament elections.

The economy

'There are only two families in the world... the Haves and the Have-nots'.

Miguel de Cervantes in *Don Quixote* (1615)

For much of the 20th century, the Spanish were among the poorest people in western Europe. Farming and herding were the most important occupations, in many places yielding only a bare living. Mining, shipbuilding and other industries were largely confined to the north and Catalonia.

The outcome of the Spanish Civil War hindered economic growth. After 1939 Franco adopted a policy of **autarky** – making Spain as self-sufficient as possible instead of trading with other nations. Wages were kept low and strikes were forbidden. The economy stagnated, and for decades, living standards remained lower than they had been in the early 1930s.

The failure of his economic policies made Franco change course in the late 1950s. Economic specialists were put in charge, and businesses were allowed greater freedom. Dramatic advances were made in the 1960s

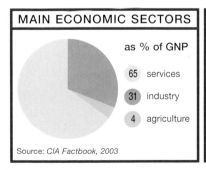

MAIN ECONOMIC SECTORS

as % of GNP

65 services
31 industry
4 agriculture

Source: *CIA Factbook, 2003*

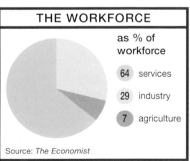

THE WORKFORCE

as % of workforce

64 services
29 industry
7 agriculture

Source: *The Economist*

Olive groves such as these are a familiar sight in Andalusia. Spain is the world's largest producer of olives and olive oil.

and particularly after Franco's death in 1975, as Spain became more fully integrated into the global economy. The labour force became free to form trade unions, and living standards rose steadily.

MAIN ECONOMIC SECTORS

In the recent past, there have been shifts in the relative importance of different economic sectors. Throughout the 20th century, large numbers of Spaniards left the countryside for work in the cities. Consequently, agriculture employs a smaller workforce and plays a smaller part in the overall economy than it did in the past. As in many other countries, by the 1980s, long-established heavy industries such as mining were also declining. By contrast, the demand for consumer goods expanded, and the leading place in the economy was taken by service industries – enterprises that involve providing a

HOW SPAIN USES ITS LAND

Crop land and forest account for much of Spain's land use. The principal crops are cereals, grapes, citrus fruits and olives, while the forest industry produces much of the world's cork. Pasture land is used mostly for grazing sheep.

crop land

forest

pasture

mountain

service rather than making something. Typical of this new economy were the ever-growing number of cafés, bars and shops in the cities and the multibillion pound tourist industry. In the early 21st century, service industries represent 65 per cent of Spain's **gross national product** (GNP). Industry still accounts for about one-third, but agriculture has shrunk to 4 per cent.

Agriculture and fishing

Spain is not rich in natural resources, and large areas are arid or prone to drought if they are not irrigated. Agriculture plays a smaller role in the Spanish economy than it did in the past. However, it is still a major sector and its yield has improved as a result of modernization and the application of high-tech methods.

Many traditionally arid areas have become productive thanks to irrigation schemes, often assisted by grants from the **European Union** (EU). In particular, horticulture (growing fruit, vegetables and flowers) has greatly expanded. Among the fruits and vegetables grown in Spain are onions, tomatoes, peppers, cucumbers, oranges, melons, peaches, apples, lemons, limes, peas, pomegranates, apricots and almonds. Bananas are the most important crop grown on the Canary Islands, which also produce coffee, dates and sugar cane. Groves of olive trees cover large areas of central and southern Spain; the country is the world's largest producer of olives and olive oil (see box on page 82). An even larger area is given over to growing grapes. Spain is third in the world among wine producers (behind Italy and France).

Traditional field crops are still important to the economy. About 20 million tonnes (19.7 million tons) of barley, wheat and other cereals are harvested every year. Substantial amounts of sugarbeet, potatoes, sunflower seeds and rice are also grown.

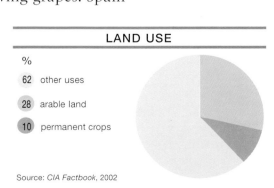

LAND USE

%

62 other uses

28 arable land

10 permanent crops

Source: *CIA Factbook*, 2002

Spain's olive oil

Spain produces more olive oil than any other country. Its annual output represents 45% of the global total, and it is also the greatest exporter. Long a staple of Mediterranean cooking, olive oil has become increasingly popular in wealthy countries where consumption of fried foods has caused health problems. In particular, olive oil is free of cholesterol, a type of fat that clogs the arteries, causing heart disease.

The superior quality of Spanish olive oil has been known since ancient times, and the Romans imported it in huge quantities. There are many varieties, each native to a given region. In recent years, subsidies (grants) from the EU have encouraged Spanish farmers to plant more olive trees and further increase production. In some places, this has led to erosion of the topsoil and fears of long-term damage.

Livestock raised include cattle, sheep, goats, pigs, chickens, horses, asses and mules.

In the past, the seas around the mainland were rich in fish, but the depletion of stocks threatens to become a serious problem. Spain's commercial fishing fleet is one of the largest in the world; in Europe, it is second only

to Denmark's. Most of Spain's fishing fleet is based in the north-west and in Andalusia, and the largest catches are of sardines, and skipjack and yellowfin tuna.

Manufacturing, mining and construction

Spain's oldest manufactures were craft products such as leather goods, lace, textiles, ceramics, glass, silverwork and musical instruments. These were all originally made by hand and required considerable skill and experience. Some handicrafts survive – textiles remain a major industry – but many goods are now machine made and are often directed mainly at the tourist market.

Large-scale manufacturing began in the 19th century and took the form of heavy industries such as coal and iron-mining, iron and steel production, shipbuilding, textiles and chemical production. These industries still exist, although they are less important in the overall economy. Mining operations now extend to zinc, lead, copper, tungsten, lignite, uranium and other minerals.

These fishing boats are hauling in a catch of tuna in Andalusian waters. Overfishing has had a severe impact on fish stocks, leading to EU restrictions that protect declining stocks. Today, the industry is shrinking and its future is uncertain.

This hydroelectric dam is in the Sierra de Guara in Aragon. Hydroelectricity accounts for 18 per cent of Spain's energy.

Spain's older industries have been overtaken by the manufacture of cars and other vehicles. Vehicle production has reached 3 million units a year, representing almost 7 per cent of the GNP. By comparison, the figure for mining is 1 per cent. Spain is currently the world's fifth-largest manufacturer of vehicles.

ENERGY SOURCES

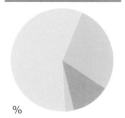

%

50　oil, gas, coal and diesel

27　nuclear

18　hydroelectricity

5　other

source: *CIA World Factbook*

Energy

Spain's coal reserves, though large, are generally of a low quality, and some coal has to be imported. Natural gas and petroleum deposits are small, and these have to be imported in substantial quantities – gas mainly from Libya and Algeria, and petroleum from Mexico. Spanish governments have made strenuous efforts to diversify production in order to reduce the country's dependence on imports. Almost half of Spain's electricity needs are now supplied by nuclear or hydroelectric power. Spain has also become a leader in the development of a new technology, wind power.

MAJOR INDUSTRIES

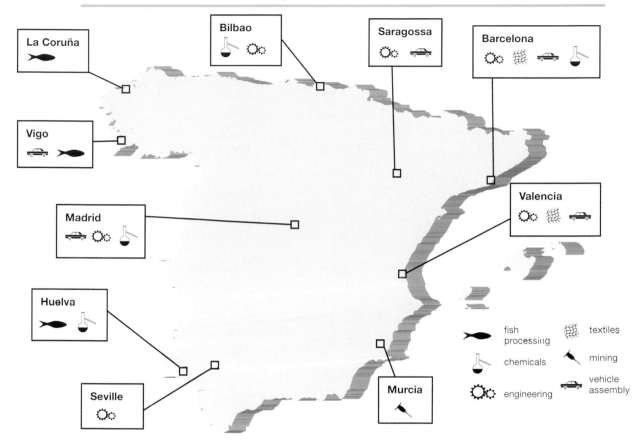

The construction industry plays a significant role in the economy, thanks to ambitious development schemes in the big cities and constant construction projects in the coastal tourist areas.

Other important Spanish industries include oil-refining, food-processing (mostly fish), machine tools engineering and the manufacture of electronic goods and footwear.

Service industries

Service industries – such as the hotel trade, education and welfare – provide services rather than goods. As in other economically advanced countries, the service sector has expanded to become much more important than

Tourism

Until the 1960s, tourism made little contribution to the Spanish economy. Little of the country was known to outsiders, and the poverty of the population meant that Spanish holidaymakers spent very little money. Then Spain, cheap and sunny, began to attract the attention of holidaymakers from other, rapidly prospering European countries. Mass tourism developed along with the provision of cheap flights and package holidays, in which travel firms arrange both flights and accommodation. Millions of people who had never been abroad could now travel with confidence. The Spanish responded by building huge numbers of high-rise hotels and apartment blocks along the coasts, which became accessible through conveniently located airports.

Expansion has continued ever since, although some efforts have been made to improve the appearance of densely built-up areas and to limit the considerable environmental damage done by rapid high-rise building.

The sunshine and beaches of the coasts and the islands are still the principal attraction for about 80% of visitors. But increasing numbers are drawn to other aspects of Spain, including the culture and nightlife of Madrid and Barcelona, festivals and processions in other historic cities and the outdoor pleasures of national parks and the green north-west.

Almost 50 million overseas tourists visit Spain each year. Earnings from tourism exceed £18,750 million and account for more than 10% of GNP.

other sectors. In Spain, service industries account for 65 per cent of economic activity. An unusually large and vital part is played by a single service industry, tourism (see box on opposite page). The majority of overseas tourists are from the UK and Germany.

The workforce

The Spanish workforce numbers about 17 million people. Fewer than a million now work in the traditional occupations, agriculture and fishing. Manufacturing, mining and the construction industry employ over 4.25 million people. The rest work in the service industries. In 2002, more than 11 per cent of those available for work were unemployed, and unemployment remains one of Spain's most serious problems.

Only 20 per cent of the workforce are members of trade unions, a very low figure by European standards. In the late 1970s, government, employers and unions worked together closely to make **democracy** a success, but the unions opposed the austerity (belt-tightening) measures imposed to help Spain become a member of the EU in 1986. Since then, unemployment, **privatization** and other issues have prompted strike action, including a general strike in mid-2002. The majority of Spanish unions belong to one of two federations. The Workers' Commissions is linked with left-wing political parties, and the General Union of Workers is affiliated to the centre-left Spanish Socialist Workers' Party (PSOE).

Foreign trade

Spain always imports more goods than it exports. The imbalance could be serious, but it is more or less made up by 'invisible' exports – activities that bring in foreign currency. This is why a flourishing tourist industry is so vital to the country's prosperity. Foreign investment in Spain is another important source of income.

The chief Spanish exports are machinery, cars (about 17 million), chemical products, textiles and agricultural

MAIN FOREIGN ARRIVALS

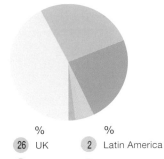

%		%	
26	UK	2	Latin America
23	Germany	44	other Europe
2	USA	3	other

source:
Government of Spain

EXPORTS (£000m)		IMPORTS (£000m)	
raw materials	30.9	raw materials	43.4
consumer goods	27.9	consumer goods	23.5
capital goods	9.4	capital goods	17.2
energy products	2.5	energy products	11.6
total (including others)	70.9	total (including others)	95.7

source: *The Economist*

Spain's main trading partners are France and Germany, with other EU countries not far behind.

MAIN TRADING PARTNERS

EXPORTS

%
20 France
12 Germany
10 Portugal
9 Italy
49 others

IMPORTS

%
17 France
16 Germany
9 Italy
7 Benelux countries
51 others

source: *CIA Factbook*

products such as olives, olive oil, wine and citrus fruits. Imports include a wide range of manufactured goods, machinery (including electrical and nuclear equipment), petroleum, chemicals and consumer goods.

About one-third of Spanish trade is conducted with either France or Germany. Substantial trade also takes place between Spain and Italy, Portugal, Belgium and the UK. Outside the EU, Latin American countries and the USA are the most important trade partners.

TRANSPORTATION

Until the 19th century, Spain's economic development was held back by poor transport links. Mountain ranges formed barriers to transport, and Spanish rivers were not navigable by craft of any great size. In the mid-19th century, the coming of the railways marked the beginning of improved communications. Since the 1960s, new road and rail facilities have put Spain on a level with other western European countries.

Road and rail

The major road network is essentially radial, with Madrid as the central point of the system. There are 347,000 kilometres (215,550 miles) of motorways, dual carriageways and other roads, carrying about three-quarters of Spain's freight. Most families own at least one car, and 90 per cent of passenger

The environment

Both the economy and the quality of Spanish life are threatened by pollution and various other forms of environmental damage. Toxic industrial waste, traffic fumes, soil erosion and the overuse of pesticides are familiar evils in most advanced economies. Spain has tended to be slow in taking action over many issues, although some big cities have schemes to reduce car use by improving railway services and introducing priority lanes for vehicles carrying more than one passenger.

A specifically Spanish problem is drought. In addition to ordinary consumer demand, extensive irrigation schemes greatly reduce the volume of water in the rivers.

Tourist facilities are a major source of coastal pollution, but this problem is difficult to tackle effectively because of the vital role played by the tourist industry. In 2002, Majorca introduced an environmental tax, payable by tourists, but it was later phased out.

Some forms of pollution arrive suddenly. In 2002, the oil tanker *Prestige* sprang a leak in stormy Atlantic waters, broke in two and sank. About 38,000 tonnes (37,400 tons) of oil were spilt and coated most of the Galician coastline. Apart from the damage to wildlife and habitats, the disaster closed hundreds of kilometres of coast to fishing and shellfish-gathering, putting more than 20,000 people out of work.

traffic is by road. Congestion and pollution are the main problems on Spain's roads.

The growth of car travel and road haulage led to a steep decline in railway use and line closures. However, services are being improved by the introduction of high-speed trains on intercity lines. These are served by the fast, comfortable Talgo trains. A separate high-speed service, the Tren de Alta Velocidad Español (AVE), links Madrid with Cordoba and Seville. Spain has about 14,200 kilometres (8880 miles) of track. The state-owned system is being modified to allow private operators to use the rail infrastructure.

Other Spanish railway networks include the underground systems of Madrid, Barcelona and Bilbao, and light railways in Valencia, Bilbao and Malaga.

Spain's AVE high-speed trains have a sleek design that enables them to easily reach speeds of 350 km/h (215 mph). There are plans for the network to connect with Barcelona and link up with the French high-speed trains.

TRANSPORTATION

All roads and railway lines radiate from the capital, Madrid. Spain has an efficient and fast rail network, with direct trains from Madrid to Paris (France) and Lisbon (Portugal), as well as from Barcelona to Paris, Zürich (Switzerland), Milan (Italy) and Geneva (Switzerland).

——————— major roads
+++++++ railways
——————— major rivers
✈ major airports

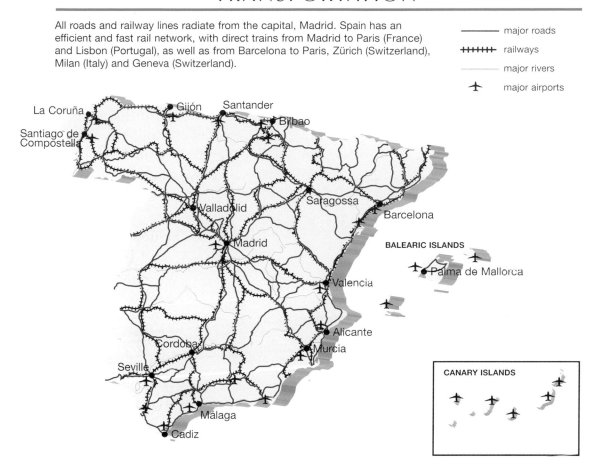

BALEARIC ISLANDS

CANARY ISLANDS

Sea and air

Spain has ports on both the Atlantic and Mediterranean coasts, and maritime trade has always been an important part of the Spanish economy. The Spanish merchant marine is one of the largest in the world, comprising about 1540 vessels carrying freight between Spain and other countries.

Mainland Spain has eighteen international airports. There are also three on the Balearic Islands and five on the Canaries. Barajas, Madrid, is Spain's busiest airport for both passenger traffic and freight. Iberia is the state-owned national airline. Its principal national competitors are Air Europa and Spanair.

Arts and living

'In Spain, the dead are more alive than the dead of any other country in the world'.

Spanish poet Federico García Lorca (1898–1936)

In recent times, the Spanish way of life has changed dramatically. Until the 1960s, Spain was economically behind and played little part in European life. Ideas, artistic styles and fashions crossed the Pyrenees with some difficulty and were not always welcomed in Spain. Decades of a dictatorship, widely despised by the outside world, only added to Spanish isolation.

The new Spain is different in almost every respect. Although some remote areas remain relatively poor, the grinding poverty of the past has largely disappeared. Spaniards' experience of working abroad, and of playing host to millions of tourists, has ended Spain's cultural isolation. Most Spaniards are happy with the country's role in the **European Union** (EU), and modern communications such as television ensure that European trends can be picked up almost overnight.

Modernization has affected life at the most basic level. Previously, Spain had a high birth rate and a high death rate, a pattern typical of traditional societies. Now, better health care means Spaniards are living much longer. Fewer are marrying, however, and the birth rate has fallen even more sharply. Large families are now the exception, and more resources are invested in children. As well, improvements in the educational system give these children a wider outlook and greater opportunities to improve their lives.

Traditional coffee houses, such as this one in Barcelona, sell not only coffee but also a delicious array of sweets, pastries and cakes.

93

Spaniards are now part of modern international culture, whether it takes the form of TV programmes, films, music, fast food or adventure sports. Changing values have led some people to challenge certain Spanish traditions, such as bullfighting, but most Spaniards remain attached to their cultural heritage.

THE ARTS

Spain's rich cultural heritage is most visible in the historic buildings and old quarters of so many Spanish towns and cities. It is also to be found in the precious masterpieces of Spanish literature and art.

Literature

Spanish-born authors, writing in Latin, made important contributions to Roman literature. Later, Moorish and Jewish poets and philosophers wrote extensively in Arabic and Hebrew.

Written records of poetry and prose in Castilian Spanish, Catalan and Gallego (Galician) first appear in the **Middle Ages**. The best-known early medieval work is the Spanish epic *Cantar del mío Cid* (*Song of the Cid*), a 12th-century poem of 3730 lines about a national hero, El Cid (see box on page 60). The medieval Spanish heritage included poetry, moralistic prose tales and tales of **chivalry** and romance such as *Amadis of Gaul*. The romances featured **knights errant** who, serving their chosen lady, killed giants and monsters.

The 16th- and 17th-century Golden Age brought new literary forms and Spain's most revered writers. The author of *Lazarillo de Tormes* (1554) remains unknown, yet the story marks the beginning of a European tradition – the **picaresque** novel, which describes a roguish hero's wanderings and adventures. These novels portrayed the social scene, often with some satire.

The most famous work in Spanish literature, *Don Quixote* (two parts, 1605 and 1615), was, among other things, a satire, making fun of chivalrous romances such

Miguel de Cervantes (1547–1616)

The most famous Spanish book, *Don Quixote*, was written by Miguel de Cervantes. He led an adventurous life as a young man, fighting against the Turks at the Battle of Lepanto, where he was wounded and lost the use of his left arm. Returning to Spain from Italy in 1575, he was captured by Turkish pirates and was a prisoner for five years. Back in Spain, he could not find a job and turned increasingly to writing.

Cervantes' novel *Don Quixote*, first published in 1605, soon became immensely popular. Its central character is an elderly man who has read so many knightly romances that he can no longer tell the difference between reality and imagination. Deciding to become a knight errant, he recruits Sancho Panza, a peasant, as his attendant and chooses a farm girl as the 'lady' for whom he will perform great deeds.

The lean, mad Don Quixote goes forth with his plump, down-to-earth attendant and falls into a series of comic misadventures. In one episode, Don Quixote is convinced that a group of windmills are evil giants. He charges against them, with terrible results. Mixing comedy, tragedy and social comment, *Don Quixote* was a key work in the development of the novel.

as *Amadis*. Its author, Miguel de Cervantes (1547–1616; see box on page 95), wrote many other stories, poems and plays.

The Golden Age also produced two great Spanish dramatists. Lope de Vega (1562–1635) wrote hundreds of plays and many poems, usually on typically Spanish themes of love and honour. Pedro Calderón de la Barca (1600–81) examined Spanish values at a time when the country was beginning to decline.

Among the great poets of the Golden Age were Garcilaso de la Vega (1501–36), Luis de Góngora (1561–1627) and Francisco de Quevedo (1580–1645). The intense religious feelings of the period are reflected in the mystical writings of two figures, St Teresa of Avila (1515–82) and the poet St John of the Cross (1542–91).

After a long period in which Spanish literature followed European trends, a major figure appeared in the 19th century. In two long cycles of novels, Benito Pérez Galdós (1843–1920) created a panorama of recent history and an encyclopaedic account of society.

Spanish writers reacted strongly to their country's humiliation in the war of 1898 against the USA. Modern styles and ideas reached Spain through the works of the philosopher Miguel de Unamuno (1864–1936), the poet Antonio Machado (1875–1939) and others who are often labelled 'the generation of '98'. One of Spain's greatest modern poets, Federico García Lorca (1898–1936), became internationally known at the end of the 1920s (see box opposite). He was murdered by Nationalists for his outspoken

Don Juan

A fictional Spanish character, Don Juan, has often featured in the European arts as 'the great lover'. He first appeared in a play, *El Burlador de Sevilla* (*The Trickster of Seville*, about 1630), by the Spanish writer Tirso de Molina. Here, he is just a wicked young nobleman, condemned to be dragged down to hell. But subsequently he was interpreted in different ways by, among others, the 17th-century French playwright Molière, the Austrian composer Mozart (in the opera *Don Giovanni*, 1787) and the Irish playwright G. B. Shaw (*Man and Superman*, 1903).

Federico García Lorca (1898–1936)

Federico García Lorca was born just outside Granada, in Andalusia. He developed a style of poetry that was modern but also saturated with the exotic side of Andalusian tradition, such as folklore, Gypsy life and flamenco. After his 'Gypsy ballads', *Romancero gitano* (1929), made him famous, Lorca lived for a time in New York. On his return, he became involved in the popular theatre movement that developed under the new Spanish **Republic**, and he wrote *Blood Wedding* (1933) and other plays. At the outbreak of the Spanish Civil War in 1936, Lorca was in Granada, where he was shot dead by **Nationalists**.

left-wing views at the start of the Spanish Civil War in 1936. After Franco's victory, many Spanish writers went into exile.

During Franco's dictatorship, censorship put strict limits on what those writers who remained in Spain were able to express, and writing in Catalan and Gallego, which had been revived in the 19th century, was again suppressed. However, Camilo José Cela (1916–2002), who had fought on the Nationalist side, published novels such as *The Family of Pascal Duarte* (1942) and *The Hive* (1951), which gave a brutally realistic picture of Spanish life. Cela was awarded the 1989 Nobel Prize for literature.

Since 1975, Spanish literary life has flourished. No one main figure has emerged, but many works have been published by both male and female writers and in all the country's languages.

Art

The long tradition of art in Spain begins with prehistoric paintings on rock surfaces, notably in the caves at Altamira (see box on page 52). Many stone and bronze figurines have been discovered that date from the last few centuries BC. The most remarkable and best-preserved sculpture is a bust, nicknamed *The Lady of Elche* (see page 54), in which a classically severe face is framed by a highly ornamental headdress and costume.

Much Roman and Visigothic art has vanished, but Islamic Spain has left a rich legacy. **Islam** frowned on figurative art – that is, representations of human beings and the world. So Islamic artists developed a fantastically intricate decorative art that sometimes has an almost hypnotic effect. Surfaces were covered with dazzlingly coloured geometric and floral shapes, flowing, looping lines (arabesques) and calligraphy – Arabic script, used for decorative purposes. Many of the most famous examples were used on buildings – for example, on tiles (*azulejos*) and in plasterwork. Moorish craftsmen also practised a range of crafts, including metalwork, ceramics and woodcarving.

Painting in medieval Christian Spain mainly took the form of illuminated manuscripts (books with painted illustrations) and murals (wall paintings) in churches. Many of the best were done in Catalonia, which was most open to European influence. In the work of Pedro Berruguete (*c.*1450–1504), medieval styles began to give way to the greater realism of the Italian **Renaissance**. Berruguete, who may have worked in Italy, became court painter to Ferdinand and Isabella (see page 61).

Spain's Golden Age was an artistic as well as a political and literary peak. However, the first great artist in the Spanish tradition was a foreigner, El Greco (1541–1614; see box opposite). His unearthly religious painting was followed by the more human art of Francisco Ribalta (1565–1628) and that of José de Ribera (1591–1652).

The artist José de Ribera settled in Naples in Italy in 1616, where he was known as Lo Spagnoletto (the Little Spaniard).

The Golden Age was beginning to lose its glitter during the lifetime of Diego Velázquez (1599–1660), one of the greatest Spanish painters. He was born in Seville, where his paintings of everyday life showed his technical skill and profound insight into people. These qualities enabled him to make a successful career at the court in Madrid. He was supreme as a portraitist, although Pope Innocent X complained that Velázquez was 'too truthful'. His work ranged from a great historical scene, *The Surrender of Breda* (before 1635), to his greatest masterpiece, *Las Meninas* (*The Maids of Honour*, c.1656; see photograph on page 100).

Two other important figures worked during the Golden Age. Francisco de Zurbarán (1598–1664) painted sombre studies of monks and saints. Bartolomé Murillo (1618–82) developed a softer, more popular style, both for religious subjects and sentimental studies of street urchins.

After a long interval, another towering artistic figure appeared. The painter

El Greco (1541–1614)

One of the most remarkable figures in Spanish art was born far away from Spain, on the Greek island of Crete, and only settled in Toledo when he was about 36. The Spanish called him El Greco (The Greek), the name by which he is now always known. His real name – which he signed on all his paintings – was Domenikos Theotokopoulos.

With very few exceptions, El Greco's paintings were of religious scenes, often intended for altars. They were painted in a strange personal style, with elongated figures and intense, disturbing, highlighted colours. The emotionally elated, mystical atmosphere is seen in such famous works as *The Burial of Count Orgaz* (seen here), *The Agony in the Garden* and *Christ Stripped of His Garments*.

Francisco de Goya (1746–1828) had an astounding range. Early in his career, he designed tapestries for the royal family in a light-hearted style. As the court portraitist, he could be as unflattering as Velázquez. Then he became deaf after a serious illness, and much of his work took on a fearful, even nightmarish quality. The savage war against the French prompted a fearful collection of engravings, *The Disasters of War*, as well as paintings of the Second and Third May rising in Madrid (see pages 41 and 70). In his final years, Goya painted terrible visions – called the 'Black Paintings' – on the walls of his own house.

During the 20th century, several Spaniards contributed to the revolutionary art movements of the period. Pablo Picasso (1881–1973) is widely regarded as the greatest artist of the century. He was born in Málaga, spent his early years in Barcelona and lived for the rest of his life in France. Picasso painted his famous *Guernica* to protest against an atrocity carried out by Franco's German allies in the Spanish Civil War. After

Franco's victory in the Civil War, Picasso remained in permanent exile. He had incredible natural gifts, moving effortlessly from one style to the next. He was one of the founders of cubism, a style of art in which reality is represented by geometric shapes. A younger Spaniard, Juan Gris (1887–1927), remained a cubist, but Picasso continued to move on until the end of his life, producing original work as a printmaker, sculptor and potter, as well as many paintings.

Dali's surreal theatre

The Dali Theatre-Museum in Figueras is one of Spain's most bizarre and popular artistic attractions. Figueras was the birthplace of the painter Salvador Dali, who bought the town's theatre and, from 1961 onwards, turned it into a kind of temple dedicated to himself – he is even buried in it. The building is painted wine-red on the outside and crowned with enormous egg-like shapes. The interior is equally extraordinary, including a room entitled 'The Face of Mae West', an American film star of the 1930s. Seen from the staircase above, the furnishings look like a portrait of the actress. One of Dali's most celebrated creations is a scarlet couch with wave-like sides, representing Mae West's full, red lips.

Picasso was briefly associated with surrealism, a style of art that attempted to tap the unconscious mind. This produced strange and disturbing images, typical of the work of Salvador Dali (1904–89). Dali used a conventional technique with a high finish, which gave a photographic quality to his works. His showmanship made him a celebrity, especially in the USA.

Other 20th-century Spanish artists include the painters Joan Miró (1893–1983), Antoni Tàpies (born 1923) and Antonio Saura (born 1930), and the sculptor Eduardo Chillida (born 1924).

Architecture

Spain has significant Roman remains such as the **aqueduct** at Segovia and the bridge at Alcántara. A handful of Visigothic churches also survive. In the ninth century, graceful churches were built in the Asturias, but their original Spanish style was abandoned when the **Romanesque** style arrived from France. Many Spanish cathedrals and other buildings were built in the bulky, round-arched Romanesque style and its successor, the soaring, Gothic pointed-arch style which was also an import from France.

Meanwhile, Islamic Spain developed its own distinctive style. Much was destroyed by the **Moors**' Christian conquerors, but major buildings survive. The most famous of these are the Mezquita (Great Mosque) of Cordoba (8th–10th centuries); La Giralda (12th century)

and the Torre del Oro (13th century), both in Seville; and the Alhambra of Granada (11th–14th centuries) (see pages 48–9).

A number of Moorish castles (*alcázars*) also survive, including the Alcázar of Seville (see page 46). Spain soon had many castles, for Christian nobles also built them during the Middle Ages. Pedro the Cruel had a palace constructed within the Seville Alcázar, employing a Moorish workforce. Such a mixing of cultures led to the creation of two purely Spanish architectural styles: **Mudéjar**, in which the construction was done by Moors working under Christian rule, and Mozarabic, done by Christians who had adopted Moorish culture.

L'Eixample (The Extension), a district of Barcelona, contains many examples of modernista architecture, including Antoni Gaudí's Casa Batlló. Its wavy balconies and window frames and multi-coloured walls give it the appearance of an undersea castle.

Early in the 16th century, Gothic buildings became highly ornamented, in a distinctively Spanish style known as **plateresque**. New styles continued to arrive from abroad, and Spanish architecture alternated between an ornamented style and one that used little or no ornament. The Italian Renaissance reintroduced the round arch and insisted upon symmetry. The Palace of Charles V within the Alhambra, in Granda, was an early example, but austerity triumphed in the plain but overpowering vastness of Herrera's El Escorial, the royal palace outside Madrid (see box on page 40). The arrival of the baroque style, with its sweeping lines and sense of drama, encouraged Spanish architects to use masses of ornament again, this time in a style known (after two architect brothers) as Churrigueresque.

In the 18th century, substantial building was done in the relatively sober **neo-classical** style. Spanish exuberance broke out again between 1880 and 1910, when the *modernista* movement created a highly original architecture in Catalonia. The outstanding figure, Antoni Gaudí (1852–1926) combined sound structural practice with extraordinary decorative schemes. His most ambitious project, La Sagrada Família (Holy Family) church in Barcelona, begun in the 1880s, is still being built.

During the 20th century, political upheavals limited the development of architecture. From 1982, however, building programmes were undertaken on an unprecedented scale, especially for the 1992 Barcelona Olympics and Seville World Expo.

There have also been many less publicized schemes of rebuilding and refurbishment that have transformed Spain's cities and small towns. Architecture is now internationalized, and Spaniards such as Rafael Moneo (born 1937) and Ricardo Bofill (born 1939) work both at home and abroad. Equally, major projects in Spain have been undertaken by foreign architects such as Britain's Norman Foster and the American Frank Gehry. The latter's **titanium** Guggenheim Museum in Bilbao is widely considered to be the finest of all contemporary buildings (see photograph right).

Music and dance

Although Spain has a rich heritage of folk music, there were few classical composers of note before the 20th century, perhaps because the country was cut off from the main European tradition. In the 19th century, there was a fashion for all things Spanish, especially among French writers, painters and composers, who thought the Spanish were more passionate and exotic than their neighbours. The popular

The inspiration behind Frank Gehry's Guggenheim Museum, which opened in 1997, was the anatomy of a fish and a boat hull. The titanium and glass used in its construction reflect the light in different colours and are meant to resemble fish scales.

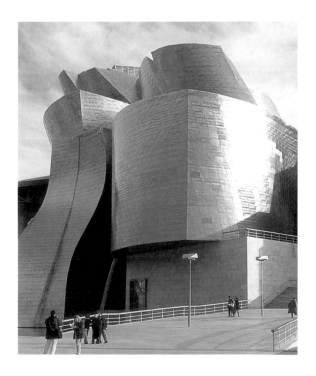

*These flamenco
students are dancing
in Tenerife, the Canary
Islands. Although
flamenco originates in
Andalusia, flamenco
music and dance are
performed in many
parts of Spain.*

music of Andalusia inspired Frenchman Georges Bizet to compose his famous opera *Carmen* (1873–74), whose Gypsies, bandits and bullfighters created an image of Spain that has fascinated generations of music lovers. A similar spirit lay behind many pieces by Spain's own best-known composer, Manuel de Falla (1876–1946).

Among other Spanish composers of note were Enrique Granados (1867–1916) and Isaac Albéniz

Flamenco

Flamenco is the music of Spain's Gypsies, most of whom lived in Andalusia originally. Its best-known version is *cante hondo* (deep song). This singing is accompanied by one or more dancers, whose large gestures, finger-snapping and rhythmically stamping heels have a hypnotic effect. The performance often builds slowly to an explosive climax. Gypsy family ties are very strong, which has helped to preserve the authentic tradition over the years. Diluted versions of flamenco are often staged for tourist audiences.

(1860–1909), who were both piano virtuosos, and Joaquín Rodrigo (1901–99). Another great instrumentalist was the cellist Pablo Casals (1876–1973). In recent times, some of the world's leading operatic stars have been Spaniards, including the tenors Placido Domingo (born 1941) and José Carreras (born 1946), and the soprano Montserrat Caballé (born 1933).

Some folk traditions survive, such as the bagpipe music of Galicia. It is flamenco music, though, that has come to symbolize Spain and is performed everywhere, though it is native to Andalusia (see box opposite).

The film industry

Some of the finest film directors have been Spanish, despite the heavy censorship of the Franco period and Spain's inability to compete with the resources of Hollywood. Luis Buñuel (1900–83) had a remarkable career. In Paris, he collaborated with the artist Salvador Dali to make two famous surrealist films, *Un Chien Andalou* (1928) and *L'Age d'Or* (1930). After the Spanish Civil War, he worked in obscurity in the USA. He re-emerged in the 1950s with a number of films made in Mexico, after which *Viridiana* (1961) and other powerful and bizarre works brought him international recognition.

Juan Bardem (1922–2002), Luis Berlanger (born 1921) and Carlos Saura (born 1932) were respected directors who suffered under censorship. Bardem was actually in prison at a time when he was due to accept an international award.

Censorship was quickly relaxed after the end of the Franco era, and a new generation of filmmakers emerged. The greatest impact was made by Pedro Almodóvar (born 1951). His films have won numerous awards, including Oscsars for *Women on the Verge of a Nervous Breakdown* (1987) and *Talk to Her* (2002). Performers closely linked with Almodóvar included Carmen Maura, Victoria Abril and Antonio Banderas, who went on to international stardom.

HOW SPANIARDS SPEND THEIR MONEY

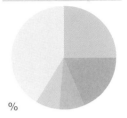

%	
41	other
25	housing
19	food
8	household expenses
7	clothing and footwear

source: Spanish National Statistics Institute

EVERYDAY LIFE

Today, Spain is in most respects a typical Western country. Most Spaniards live in lively but car-choked cities and their busy lives are often fuelled by fast food. All the same, there are still a number of features found only in Spain or, at any rate, Mediterranean countries. For the visitor, a striking feature is the Spanish hours of business. Shops open in the morning and (with the exception of cafés and bars) shut in the middle of the day for two or three hours. They reopen around 4 p.m. and continue trading until about 8 p.m. This long 'lunch hour' allows people to have a leisurely lunch and avoid working during the hottest part of the day.

Traditionally, lunch was followed by a siesta (nap), but this custom is disappearing now that many people commute to work and can escape the heat thanks to air-conditioning. A good many firms, especially those dealing with northern European and American customers, now do 'nine-to-five' hours.

Going out for a stroll or meeting up with friends in the cool of the evening is a Mediterranean tradition that many Spaniards enjoy. Even at midnight, some cities and towns are still busy with people.

WHAT DO SPANIARDS OWN?

99.7%	90%	75%	42%	37%
television	telephone	car	mobile telephone	computer

Source: Government of Spain

Spain has its own cuisine, influenced by the different cultures that have existed on the peninsula. Its moving festivals are another product of its history. And although Spaniards are fans of rock and pop music and international sports, they also remain faithful to flamenco singing and dancing and the controversial ritual of the bullfight.

Leisure and sport

Meeting in cafés or bars and strolling in the cool of the evening are Mediterranean traditions that Spaniards continue to follow. However, this practice has been modified by the lure of shopping, car trips and watching TV. Spanish television offers a familiar mixture of game shows, quizzes and soap operas. A large number of programmes are US imports, but South American soaps are also popular. Young people in the cities revel in their night life, and many people spend their holidays on the beach or in the mountains.

The bullring

Bullfighting in Spain is centuries old. By the 19th century, it had become a spectator sport, taking place in an open-air arena. The matador (principal bullfighter) is usually a man, but a few women have entered the ring.

There are three basic phases. In the first, the matador shows his skill, luring the bull to attack by waving his cape. The bull follows the moving cape, which draws him close to the matador's body. When this display is over, the bull is weakened by being wounded with pikes by men on horseback and with darts by agile men on foot. Then, after a second display with a cloth draped over a sword, the matador kills the bull. The closer the matador draws the bull to his body, the more highly his skill is rated. A quick, clean kill is also admired.

The Spanish cyclist Miguel Indurain won the world-famous road race the Tour de France for five consecutive years, from 1991 to 1995. Only one other cyclist has equalled his feat. The American Lance Armstrong won his fifth tour in 2003.

Football has the largest following of all the sports, and the Spanish club Real Madrid is one of the most famous in the world. Basketball, tennis and golf are among other popular international sports, and stars such as the golfer Severiano Ballesteros are popular heroes. Bullfighting (see box on page 109) is viewed as essentially Spanish, but many people, including Spaniards, regard it as cruel and hope to abolish it. However, it still attracts large crowds. The most distinctive regional sport is jai alai, or pelota, a Basque game rather like squash. Each player uses a hand, or a hand-held basket, to hurl the ball at a wall for the opponent to take on the rebound and return.

Health and welfare

Until the 1980s, health care was private and many poor people found it difficult to afford. Since then, Spain has created a free national health service offering first-class treatment. Private health care is still available for those who want it, and more than 6 million Spaniards have taken out private health insurance. As a result of these developments, the nation's health has improved dramatically, and life expectancy is one of the highest in the world (76 years for men, 83 for women).

Spain's other social services include unemployment benefits, old age pensions and maternity and sickness benefits. These are all funded by the government out of taxes, contributions from employers and deductions from employees' wages.

Education

Spain has created an excellent educational system in a very short time. In 1975, illiteracy (not being able to read or write) was still a problem, and children from poor families had little chance of improving their lives. Today, education between the ages of six and sixteen is free and compulsory for all. The state also funds pre-school classes for three to five-year-olds, which have proved to be immensely popular.

As well as state schools, there are many private institutions that receive government grants provided they reach a required standard. When pupils reach sixteen, they take either vocational courses (training for jobs) or entrance courses for university or college. Spain has more than 60 universities.

The school day begins around 9 a.m. and ends at about 4.30 p.m. In the hot south, some schools work through the lunch hour in order to close by about 2 p.m.

Food and drink

Spaniards eat the usual three daily meals, although snacks are also widely available in cafés and bars. Breakfast is light, consisting of coffee and a roll or pastry, or hot chocolate and a *churro* – a long strip of doughnut. Lunch is the main meal and is taken during the long midday break. Dinner is eaten at 9 p.m. or later.

EDUCATIONAL ATTENDANCE

university and college — 59%

secondary school — 94%

primary school — 100%

Source: UNESCO

How to say ...

Spanish is the language of Castile, the kingdom that created the Spanish state. It is directly descended from Latin, the language brought to Spain by the Romans. In areas where they are widely spoken, the Galician, Basque and Catalan languages have an equal status with Spanish. Street signs and menus in these languages can give the visitor some trouble, but almost everybody in the country speaks Spanish. Here are some useful Spanish words and phrases.

Please *Por favór* (pore fa-BOR)

Thank you *Gracias* (GRA-thi-as)

Yes *Sí* (SEE)

No *No* (No)

Hello *Hola* (O-la)

Goodbye *Adiós* (a-dee-OS)

Good morning *Buenos días* (bwenos DEE-ass)

Good afternoon *Buenas tardes* (bwenas TARR-dess)

Good night *Buenas noches* (bwenas NO-chess)

How are you? *¿Cómo está usted?* (KO-mo es-TA oos-ted)

I'm very well *Estoy muy bien* (es-toy mwee byen)

See you later *Hasta luego* (asta loo-aygo)

Sorry/excuse me *Perdón* (per-DON)

You're welcome *De nada* (day NA-da)

Do you speak English? *¿Habla usted inglés?* (AB-la oos-TED in-GLAYS)

I understand *Entiendo* (ent-YEN-do)

I don't understand *No entiendo* (no ent-YEN-do)

What is your name? [formal] *¿Cómo se llama?* (KO-mo say lya-ma)

What is your name? [informal] *¿Cómo te llamas?* (KO-mo tay lya-mas)

My name is ... *Me llamo ...* (may LYA-mo)

What time is it? *¿Qué hora es?* (kay ORA ess)

Mr/Sir *Señor* (sen-YOR)

Mrs/Madam *Señora* (sen-YOR-a)

Miss *Señorita* (sen-yor-ITA)

Numbers:

One *Uno/una* (OO-noh/OO-nah)

Two *dos* (DOSS)

Three *Tres* (TRAYS)

Four *Cuatro* (KWA-tro)

Five *Cinco* (THEENG-ko)

Six *Seis* (SAY-ees)

Seven *Siete* (see-AY-tay)

Eight *Ocho* (AW-choh)

Nine *Nueve* (nw-AY-bay)

Ten *Diez* (dee-ETH)

Days of the week:

Monday *Lunes* (LOO-nays)

Tuesday *Martes* (MAR-tays)

Wednesday *Miércoles* (me-YER-ko-lays)

Thursday *Jueves* (KHWAY-bays)

Friday *Viernes* (be-YER-nays)

Saturday *Sábado* (SA-ba-do)

Sunday *Domingo* (doh-MEEN-go)

Every region has its own specialities. Basque cuisine, which is based largely on seafood, has a particularly high reputation. Seafood is also popular in most other parts of Spain, and lobster, crabs, shrimp, squid and mussels appear on the menu, along with sardines, cod and tuna. Pork is the most widely eaten meat. Spaniards consume a wide range of vegetables and fruits, as well as pulses such as lentils and chickpeas.

The best known of all Spanish dishes is paella, originally a Valencian speciality but now found all over the country. It is made by frying seafood or pieces of meat with vegetables, peppers and rice. Saffron is used as a flavouring and gives paella its distinctive yellow hue.

Other national favourites are tortillas and gazpacho. Tortillas are thick, flat omelettes, eaten hot or cold and usually filled with potatoes and onions. Gazpacho is a spicy soup from Andalusia, made from tomatoes, onions, cucumbers and olive oil. It is always eaten cold or chilled with ice cubes.

Many fruits and vegetables grow abundantly in Spain, and the street markets are often the best place to buy fresh produce.

Tortilla

Unlike the Mexican tortilla, which is a round, flat bread made from cornmeal, the Spanish tortilla is a thick omelette, often served in slices as a *tapa*. The potatoes should be firm and waxy and hold their shape when cooked.

You will need:
4 large potatoes
1 large Spanish (mild) onion
125 ml (4 fl oz) olive oil
5 large eggs
salt and pepper

Method:
Peel the potatoes and onions and slice them thinly. Warm three-quarters of the oil in a heavy frying pan over a low heat. Add the potatoes and onions.

Cover the pan and cook for 30 minutes, until the vegetables are soft but not browned. Remove the vegetables with a slotted spoon and leave them to cool for about ten minutes. Pour off the excess oil in the pan. Beat the eggs in a bowl, add the potatoes and onions. Season with salt and pepper.

Warm 15 ml (1 tbsp) of fresh oil in the pan. Pour in the egg and vegetable mixture and cook gently for about ten minutes until the centre is set. Place an inverted plate over the pan. Then turn the pan over so that the half-cooked tortilla is on the plate. Warm the remaining oil in the pan. Slide in the tortilla and cook the bottom half for about five minutes. Serve in slices, either warm or cold.

The most popular snacks are *tapas*, which Spaniards eat in bars. *Tapas* range from prawns or slices of ham and spicy sausage to cheese, olives and fried mushrooms.

Fruit, crème caramel and custard (*natillas*) are popular for dessert. Spanish pastries and biscuits are rich and sweet, often made with honey and almonds or hazelnuts. Spanish drinks include sangria, red wine mixed with soda water and fruit; cava, a champagne-like drink produced in Catalonia; and sherry, which comes from Jerez de la Frontera in the south-west of Andalusia.

The media
As well as Televisión España, the state-owned station, Spain has eleven independent television companies. Cable, satellite and digital TV are all popular with viewers.

Newspapers are an important source of information and opinion. The national newspapers are all published in Madrid. *El País* has the largest circulation, with over 434,000 copies a day, followed by *El Mundo* and *ABC*. Over 80 other daily newspapers are published, with a total circulation approaching 4 million. The most widely read is Barcelona's *La Vanguardia*. The best-selling weekly publication is the gossip magazine *Pronto*, with a circulation of about 878,000.

Festivals and religion

Under Spain's 1978 constitution, there is no official state church and all faiths are tolerated. The overwhelming majority of the population (some 93 per cent) describe themselves as Roman Catholics. But some 28 per cent are Catholic in name only and do not practice any religion. The only non-Catholic group of any size are **Muslims**, mostly recent immigrants and their children, who may number as much as a million.

Most of Spain's public holidays have a religious origin. The most important day at Christmas time is 6 January (Epiphany), when presents are exchanged.

Most festivals are celebrated in a holiday spirit, with huge floats, dancing, and sometimes fireworks – as in Valencia's spectacular Las Fallas, when giant papier mâché figures are set alight. There are also many local festivals in honour of the Virgin or patron saints, including Pamplona's now internationally famous bull-running during the Festival of San Fermín.

National holidays

As well as the national holidays listed here, there are many regional and local holidays.

1 January	New Year's Day
6 January	Epiphany
March/April	Good Friday (Easter)
1 May	Labour Day
25 July	Saint James's Day
15 August	Feast of the Assumption
12 October	National Day
1 November	All Saints' Day
6 December	Constitution Day
8 December	The Immaculate Conception
25 December	Christmas Day

The future

'Europe cannot confine itself to the cultivation of its own garden'.

King Juan Carlos of Spain, addressing the United Nations in 1986

Spain has achieved a great deal in a remarkably short time. It has an advanced economy and a healthy, well-educated population. **Democracy**, though introduced only in the late 1970s, functions smoothly, enabling power to pass from one party to another without violence. Generally, the country's prospects seem excellent. However, Spain does have problems and challenges – some specific to Spain and some linked to global anxieties at the beginning of the 21st century.

Society and the economy

There is still much poverty in rural villages, particularly among older people who were left behind in the move to the towns and cities. In the cities, poor people have been driven away from the centre by the high cost of living. The unemployment rate remains high, at 11 per cent in 2003, and while some Spaniards are migrating overseas to find work, there are labour shortages in some important sectors of the economy.

These labour shortages suggest that Spain might benefit from immigration. A low birth rate and longer life expectancy mean that the Spanish are an ageing nation. A smaller and smaller workforce will have to support a constantly growing 'grey' population. This puts pressure on pensions and other benefits, and the government has recently put restrictions on some benefits.

These people are demonstrating against the Basque separatist group ETA after a bomb attack in 2000.

FACT FILE

● Unemployment remains a problem for Spain and its economy. From 1990 to 2000, the average annual unemployment rate was 19.2% (compared with 7.8% for the UK over the same period of time).

● In 2002, the people of Gibraltar voted to decide whether the UK should share **sovereignty** of the Rock with Spain. Nearly 99% of Gibraltans voted against the proposal.

● Spain ranks joint fifth in the world for the size of its eldery population (people aged 60 or over). This is proportional to the size of the workforce.

Immigration and prejudice

According to some authorities, the solution to the problem of an ageing population is to arrange for as many as 300,000 immigrants a year to enter Spain. Some 200,000 did arrive in 2000, mainly from north Africa. There is much illegal immigration from that region – many people who try to enter Spain illegally are desperate and attempt hazardous sea crossings at night. Bodies are often washed up on Spanish beaches after the failure of these dangerous and desperate attempts to start a new life in Spain.

In practice, immigration is a controversial issue, as it is in all the **European Union** (EU) countries. It is not easy to find immigrants with the kind of job and language skills required. When immigrants do arrive, they often experience considerable hostility from people who believe the newcomers will take their jobs.

More recently, there have been fears that terrorists might slip into the country alongside genuine immigrants. Such concerns fuel racial prejudice, making the situation still more tense and difficult. One short-term measure adopted by the government in 2003 was to allow the descendants of Spanish emigrants and Civil War exiles to take up citizenship. It was hoped that as many as a million people would take up the offer.

The environment

Striking a balance between immediate needs and the long-term health of the environment causes problems for many governments. Spain has its share of these, brought about by toxic waste, traffic, the burning of fossil fuels, sewage and deforestation. There are also worries about the future of agriculture, given the droughts that afflict the country from time to time and the already severe strain on water resources. Lack of water would be a particularly difficult problem to tackle if things get worse, and it could prove to be the most serious of Spain's environmental problems.

Regional tensions

Internationally, Spain seems secure as a result of its EU membership and ties with other Western countries. Gibraltar remains a divisive issue between Spain and the UK, however. While the UK seems willing to accept some form of joint sovereignty, it insists that the people of Gibraltar must agree – and the results of a referendum in 2002 made that an impossibility.

Spain is faced with the reverse situation in north Africa, where Morocco claims the towns of Ceuta and Melilla. Morocco has suggested that Gibraltar, Ceuta and Melilla might be dealt with as part of a general settlement, but Spain refuses to accept that the two issues can be treated in the same way.

Terrorism

Spain has lived with terrorism for many years. By far the most effective terrorist group has been **ETA**, which aims to achieve complete Basque independence, though neither its goals nor its methods are supported by the majority of Basques. Millions of Spaniards have taken to the streets to protest ETA outrages. In 2002 and 2003, the group targeted tourist areas in order to damage the Spanish economy.

The 2003 war in Iraq conducted by the USA, the UK and their allies, including Spain, was strongly supported by the Spanish government, but was opposed by a majority of Spaniards. For many Spaniards the mass demonstrations against government policy – like the mass demonstrations against ETA – were a sign of the healthy nature of Spanish democracy. Many Spaniards still remember the days of Franco's dictatorship, which finished only a little over 20 years ago. For them, the thronged streets of Madrid and other cities during public demonstrations are a dramatic confirmation of how fully their fellow citizens have been able to throw off political repression and enjoy the freedoms and economic advances of the democratic world.

Almanac

POLITICAL

country name:
official form: Kingdom of Spain
short form: Spain

nationality:
noun: Spaniard(s)
adjective: Spanish

official language: Castilian Spanish

capital city: Madrid

type of government:
parliamentary monarchy

suffrage (voting rights):
everyone eighteen years and over

independence: unification of kingdoms
in 1492

national anthem:
'La Marcha Real'
('The Royal March')

national holiday:
12 October (Hispanic Day)

flag:

GEOGRAPHICAL

location: south-western Europe,
bordering the Bay of Biscay,
Mediterranean Sea, North
Atlantic Ocean and Pyrenees

climate: temperate; hot summers in
interior, more moderate along
coast; cold winters in interior,
cool along coast

total area: 504,782 sq km
(194,896 sq miles)
land: 99%
water: 1%

coastline: 4964 km (3085 miles)

terrain: Pyrenees in north; large, flat
to dissected plateau surrounded
by rugged hills

highest point: Pico de Teide (Tenerife)
3718 m (12,198 ft)

lowest point: Atlantic Ocean
0 m

land use:
arable land: 28.6%
permanent crops 9.5%
other: 61.9%

natural resources: coal, lignite, iron ore, uranium, mercury, pyrites, fluorspar, gypsum, zinc, lead, tungsten, copper, kaolin, potash, hydropower, arable land

natural hazards: periodic droughts

POPULATION

population (2003 est.): 40.2 million

population growth rate (1995–2000): 0.09 %

birth rate (2003 est.): 10 births per 1000 of the population

death rate (2003 est.): 9.5 deaths per 1000 of the population

sex ratio (2003 est.): 96 males per 100 females

total fertility rate (2003 est.): 1.26 children born per woman

infant mortality rate (2003 est.): 4.54 deaths per 1000 live births

life expectancy at birth (2003 est.): total population: 79 years male: 75.9 years female: 82.8 years

literacy: total population: 97.9% male: 98.7% female: 97.2%

ECONOMY

currency: euro (€); 1€ = 100 cents

exchange rate (2003): £1 = €1.44

gross national product (2000): £3490 million

average annual growth rate (1990–2000): 2.6%

GNP per capita (2000): £8844

average annual inflation rate (1996–2001): 2.6%

unemployment rate (2003): 11%

exports (2000): £70,875 million

imports (2000): £95,687 million

foreign aid given (2000): £744 million

Human Development Index
(an index scaled from 0 to 100 combining statistics indicating adult literacy, years of schooling, life expectancy and income levels):

90.8 (UK 92.3)

TIMELINE—SPAIN

World History

Spanish History

c.50,000 BC

c.40,000 Modern humans – *Homo sapiens sapiens* – emerge

c.35,000 BC Iberians settle across much of Iberian peninsula

c.1000 BC

753 BC Foundation of Rome

492–479 BC Wars between Persia (modern-day Iran) and Greek city-states

AD 313 Constantine becomes Roman emperor and legalizes Christianity

c.1100 BC Phoenician seafarers establish trading colonies at Cadiz, in southern Spain

220–201 BC Romans defeat Carthaginians and occupy the Iberian peninsula

c.AD 400

409 Decline of Roman empire. Visigoths occupy the Iberian peninsula.

711 Muslims defeat Visigoths and occupy the Iberian peninsula

900 Vikings land in North America

c.1000

1066 The Normans conquer Britain

1348 Black Death – the plague – breaks out in Europe

1445 Gutenberg prints the first European book

1453 Turks capture Constantinople

1492 Columbus lands in America

1013 Caliphate of Cordoba weakens and breaks up. Moorish Spain splits into feuding kingdoms.

1212 Battle of Navas de Tolosa: Christian victory heralds decline of Moorish rule in Spain

1230 León and Castile unite, spearheading the Reconquest of Spain

1492 Granada, the last Moorish kingdom, falls. Expulsion of Jews and Muslims from the Iberian peninsula.

c.1500

1520 Birth of Protestantism. The pope expels Martin Luther from the Roman Catholic Church.

1620 First African slaves arrive in the Americas

1561 King Phillip II declares Madrid the capital

1588 Spanish Armada defeated en route to England

c.1700

1740–48 War of the Austrian Succession

1775–83 American War of Independence

1701–14 War of the Spanish Succession. French Bourbon dynasty comes to the throne.

2001 The World Trade Center and the Pentagon in the USA are attacked by planes flown by al-Qaeda terrorists

2000 The West celebrates the Millennium – 2000 years since the birth of Christ

2003 ETA explodes two car bombs in Spanish tourist resorts

2002 The euro replaces the peseta as the Spanish national currency

1999 Spain agrees to adopt the euro as its currency

1996 José Maria Aznar, a conservative, becomes president

1992 Barcelona hosts summer Olympics. Seville hosts Expo '92.

c.1800

1803 USA buys Louisiana from France

1824 Birth of Mexican republic

1871 Bismarck unites German states into a single country

1808–14 Peninsular War: Spaniards rebel against invading French forces

c.1900

1914–18 World War One

1933 Adolf Hitler becomes German chancellor

1939–45 World War Two

1954 Revolt breaks out in Algeria

1914–18 World War One: Spain remains neutral

1931 King Alfonso XIII abdicates. Spain is declared a republic.

1936–39 Spanish Civil War

1939–45 World War Two: Spain remains neutral

1955 Spain joins United Nations

1989 Communism collapses in eastern Europe

1969 First man lands on the Moon

1963–75 Vietnam War

c.1990

1986 Spain joins European Union

1975 Franco dies – King Juan Carlos comes to the throne

1973 ETA assassinates head of government, Luis Carrero Blanco

c.1960

Glossary

anarchism theory that all forms of government should be abolished

aqueduct bridge-like structure for carrying water

autarky economic self-sufficiency, national policy of doing without imports

Aztecs people who dominated central Mexico at the time of the Spanish conquest

baroque style of art and architecture originating in Italy in the 16th century and characterized by extravagant contrasts of light and shade and elaborate decoration

caliph/caliphate Muslim political and religious ruler; the area over which he rules

chivalry medieval system of knighthood, in which knights had certain noble qualities

coalition sharing of power or government between two or more political parties

communism political system in which goods and land are owned by everyone and there is no private property

democracy country or process in which the people choose their government by election, and in which they hold supreme power

dynasty succession of rulers belonging to the same family

elite select group or class

emir/emirate Muslim ruler; the area over which he rules

ETA Euskadi Ta Askatasuma (Basque Homeland and Freedom) terrorist group set up in 1959 to achieve Basque independence

European Union (EU) organization made up of European countries that work together on many economic, social and political issues

fascism 20th-century political movement, characterized by a rigid one-party dictatorship, suppression of opposition, nationalism and racism

Franks/Frankish Germanic tribes that established the Frankish empire, which was at its height in the 9th century

Gothic style of architecture originating in Italy in the 12th century, characterized by soaring, pointed arches

gross national product (GNP) total value of goods and services produced by the people of a country during a period, usually a year

heresy religious beliefs opposed to the official church doctrine

Incas people who dominated ancient Peru at the time of the Spanish conquest

Islam religion founded in Arabia in the 7th century and based on the teachings of Muhammad

knight-errant wandering medieval knight

Middle Ages about 1000 to 1400 AD

militia group of armed citizens, rather than professional soldiers

modernista 20th-century style of Spanish architecture, characterized by original and extraordinary decorative schemes and materials

Moors Muslim people of mixed Arab and Berber descent who invaded and occupied Spain in the 8th century AD

Mudéjar describes Muslims who lived and worked in Spain under Christian rule

Muslim follower of the teachings of Islam

Nationalists right-wing rebel forces, led by General Franco, opposed to the Republicans in the Spanish Civil War

Neanderthal a type of early human

neo-classical describes a style of architecture that revived the classical form

North Atlantic Treaty Organization (NATO) alliance of nineteen countries from North America and Europe that aims to safeguard the freedom and security of member countries by political and military means

pagan not Christian, Muslim or Jewish

parliamentary monarchy nation in which the monarch (king or queen) is the ceremonial head of state and real power lies with the head of government

picaresque type of fiction, originally from Spain, that

tells of a roguish hero's adventures

plateresque richly ornamental style that suggests silverware

privatization selling off of government-owned industries or concerns to the private sector

Reconquest advances by Christian states to recapture Spain from the Moors and unify it under Christian rule, a process that lasted several centuries

Renaissance great revival of the arts and learning in Europe during the 15th and 16th centuries that built on a rediscovery of the arts of ancient Greece and Rome

republic government in which the citizens of a country hold supreme power and where all citizens are equal under the law

Republicans left-wing government forces, opposed to the Nationalists in the Spanish Civil War

Romanesque style of architecture, dating from 11th to 13th centuries, with huge vaulting and round arches

sect followers of a particular school of thought or belief system

socialism political theory that teaches that society as a whole should be in control of a country's resources and businesses

sovereignty having independence from others, possessing supreme power

titanium silver-grey element, usually used in manufacture of aircraft

Bibliography

Major sources used for this book
Ellingham, Mark, *The Rough Guide to Spain* (Rough Guides, 2002, 10th edn)
Graff, Marie Louise, *Spain (Culture Shock! Country Guides)* (Graphic Arts Center Publishing Co., 1997)
Simonis, Damien et al., *Spain* (Lonely Planet Publications, 2003, 4th edn)
The Economist, *Pocket World in Figures* (Profile Books, 2003)

General further reading
Bennett, Lynda A. (ed.), *Encyclopedia of World Cultures* (G. K. Hall & Co., 1992)
Student Atlas (Dorling Kindersley, 1998)
The Kingfisher History Encyclopedia (Kingfisher, 1999)
The World Book Encyclopedia (Scott Fetzer Company, 1999)
World Reference Atlas (Dorling Kindersley, 2000)

Further reading about Spain
Fletcher, Richard, *Moorish Spain* (Weidenfeld and Nicholson, 2001)
Fraser, Ronald, *Blood of Spain: An Oral History of the Spanish Civil War* (Pimlico, 1994)
Hooper, John, *The New Spaniards* (Penguin, 1995)
Rodgers, Eamonn (ed.), *Encyclopedia of Contemporary Spanish Culture* (Routledge, 2001)

Some websites about Spain
CIA World Factbook
www.cia.gov/cia/publications/factbook/geos/sp.html
The Spanish Embassy in London
http://spain.embassyhomepage.com/
All About Spain, information on geography, history, cuisine and culture
www.red2000.com/spain/index-eng.html
The Guggenheim Museum
www.guggenheim-bilbao.es/idioma.htm

Index

Acknowledgements

Cover photo credits
Corbis: Kelly-Mooney Photography

Photo credits
Brown Reference Group: 8, 62; **Clare Newman:** 49, 104, 113; **Corbis:** Archivo Iconografica, S. A. 54, 60, 69, 99, 100, Christie's Images 95, Dusko Despotovic 116; **Empics:** Miguel Indurain 110; **Hutchison Picture Library:** N. Haslam 86, Jeremy Homer 92, Lesley Nelson 82, Edward Parker 6, Kerstin Rodgers 108; **John Jackson:** 28, 32, 84; **Life File Photo Library:** David Kampfner 105, Emma Lee 12, 27, 31, 56;

Mary Evans Picture Library: 63, 65, 66; **Photodisc, Inc:** Emma Lee/Life File 17, 19, 50; **Rachel Bean:** 24, 40, 101; **Robert Hunt Library:** 71, 75, 103; **Still Pictures:** John Cancalosi 89, David Drain 78, Martin Gilles 18, Michel Gunther 83; **Sylvia Cordaiy Photo Library:** Julian Worker 45; **Topham Picturepoint:** 97; **Travel Ink:** Ronald Badkin 36, Marc Dubin 25, Alec Fairbrother 106, Clive Geoffrey 38, Ken Gibson 48, 52; **Turespana:** M. Blanco 23; **www.alleuroperail.com:** 90.